The Impeachment of William Jefferson Clinton

Daniel Cohen

Twenty-First Century Books
Brookfield, Connecticut

Photographs courtesy of Liaison Agency: pp. 9, 36, 57, 83 (© Brad Markel), 35
(© Dirck Halstead), 71 (© Elizabeth Lippman); AP/Wide World Photos: p. 14,
19, 44, 97; Sygma: pp. 25 (© Woodward), 32-33, 39 (© Jamal A. Wilson), 52
(CNN), 91 (© Jamal A. Wilson); Archive Photos: pp. 80 (© Reuters/Mark
Wilson), 89 (© Official Senate Photo/CNP)

Published by Twenty-First Century Books
A Division of The Millbrook Press, Inc.
2 Old New Milford Road, Brookfield, CT   06804
www.millbrookpress.com

Library of Congress Cataloging-in-Publication Data
Cohen, Daniel, 1936–
The impeachment of William Jefferson Clinton / Daniel Cohen.
p.   cm.
Includes bibliographical references and index.
Summary: Examines the events leading to the impeachment of President Bill
Clinton, including the Whitewater investigation, the media coverage, the grand
jury proceedings, impeachment by the Senate, and the legacy of this scandal.
ISBN 0-7613-1711-2 (lib. bdg.)
1. Clinton, Bill, 1946– —Impeachment—Juvenile literature. 2. United States—
Politics   and   government—1993-   —Juvenile   literature.   3.   Trials
(Impeachment)—United States—Juvenile literature [1. Clinton, Bill, 1946– —
Impeachment. 2. Trials (Impeachment) 3. Impeachments. 4. United States—
Politics and government—1993-] I. Title.
E886.2.C64   2000   973.929'092—dc21   99-056179

JAN   8 2001

Contents

CHAPTER ONE
The Scandal Breaks
7

CHAPTER 2
The "Character Issue"
13

CHAPTER 3
Tapes
23

CHAPTER 4
Sting
31

CHAPTER 5
"You Could Go to Jail . . ."
42

CHAPTER 6

Counterattack

49

CHAPTER 7

Testimony

58

CHAPTER 8

The Report and the Reaction

69

CHAPTER 9

Impeachment

77

CHAPTER 10

Trial and the End

86

CHAPTER 11

Legacy

96

CHRONOLOGY

104

NOTES

106

BIBLIOGRAPHY

108

INDEX

110

The Impeachment of William Jefferson Clinton

1 The Scandal Breaks

It seems fitting that the biggest political scandal of late twentieth-century America should first break over the Internet.

Early on the morning of Sunday, January 19, 1998, Matt Drudge, who operated a little Internet gossip Web site from his apartment in a run-down section of Hollywood Boulevard in Santa Monica, California, posted an item on his "Drudge Report" about President Bill Clinton and a young White House intern. The intern's name wasn't given in the Drudge Report.

According to Drudge, the president had repeated sexual encounters with the intern in the White House. And, said Drudge, "tapes of intimate phone conversations exist."

Drudge did not claim to have developed this information on his own. He indicated that

Newsweek magazine had been working on the story for months and was ready to publish it, but at the last moment "spiked" (journalistic slang for killed or delayed publishing) the piece.

At the time Matt Drudge was barely known, and those who did know of him did not consider his Internet site a very reliable source of information. Drudge was an eccentric, who always wore a fedora to give himself the look of a gossip columnist of an earlier era. He started by posting Hollywood gossip and moved on to political gossip, usually with a right-wing slant. In the past he had posted stories that turned out to be spectacularly wrong.

This story was different. Reports of a relationship between a former White House intern and the president had already been making the rounds of Washington journalists and other insiders, so they had good reason to believe that the Drudge account was accurate. In many ways official Washington is a small town; people who work there always refer to it as a town rather than a city. Gossip is an ever-present fact of life in Washington, and few personal secrets remain secret for very long.

It would only have been a matter of time, and not much time either, before all the revelations would begin tumbling out. The Drudge Report opened the floodgates by making public what had already been widely discussed privately. Later that Sunday morning, the story of the president and the former intern was being discussed on ABC's *This Week*, one of the major Sunday morning television news and discussion shows.

On Tuesday *The Washington Post* came out with a much more detailed and accurate story. The *Post*

Matt
Drudge

was one of the most respected newspapers in the country, and it was not a source that could be easily dismissed.

By this time the former intern's name had been made public—Monica Lewinsky. Additional and extremely damning information had been added to the story. It was reported that fearing exposure of his relationship, the president got his friend Vernon Jordan, a powerful Washington lawyer, to find Lewinsky a well-paying job outside of Washington in order to keep her quiet.

A few days later *Newsweek* weighed in with an unprecedented thirty-page section on the story—by far the most detailed, sensational, and accurate account yet. Correspondent Michael Isikoff had been doggedly working on the story for nearly a year. *Newsweek* editors insisted that they had never spiked the story, "but given the magnitude of the allegations and the information" they wanted to hold off until they could either talk to Monica Lewinsky or spend more time assessing her credibility. When they were scooped, "it hurt like hell," confessed Editor in Chief Richard M. Smith.[1]

Suddenly the tale of the president and the White House intern was the biggest story in America, and it was to remain that for over a year. It came very close to bringing down the Clinton presidency, and it may have forever changed the way Americans think and talk about their political leaders.

The story line was an old and familiar one. A powerful man has an affair with a young female staff member. In this case the powerful man happened to be the president of the United States. The staff member was a twenty-one-year-old, Monica Lewinsky, who had started as an unpaid White House intern, moved on to a low-level White House staff job, and later worked at the Pentagon.

Sex scandals, even involving the president, were nothing new in Washington. In the late nineteenth-century, President Grover Cleveland was accused, correctly, of having fathered an illegitimate child. The revelation did not keep him from being elected. It was an open secret in Washington that President Warren G. Harding, a pillar of conservative mid-western values, had a mistress. The public at large did not know about this until after Harding's sudden and unexpected death in 1923.

President John F. Kennedy's numerous affairs were well known to the Washington press corps.

But, as Ben Bradlee, editor of *The Washington Post* said, since the affairs did not seem to affect the way JFK conducted his official duties it wasn't something the press thought they should write about, at that time.

But attitudes were slowly beginning to change. In 1971 powerful Arkansas congressman Wilbur Mills was driving too fast when Washington police stopped him. Mills was drunk (his drinking was another open but unreported Washington secret). Mills and his passenger were unhurt. His passenger, however, jumped out of the car and into the nearby tidal basin. She was a stripper who performed under the name Fannie Fox. The scandal forced Mills into retirement.

A short time later newspapers reported that Wayne Hays, another powerful congressman, had his girlfriend, Elizabeth Ray, on the public payroll. When asked about her duties Ray said famously, "I can't type, I can't file, I can't even answer the phone . . ." Hays, too, took an early retirement.

By 1987 it had become apparent that the private lives of prominent politicians were no longer off limits. The press got wind of a rumor that Colorado senator Gary Hart, a leading contender for the Democratic presidential nomination, was having an affair with a young woman named Donna Rice. Hart denied this repeatedly and practically challenged reporters to prove it. They did. The tabloid *National Enquirer* ran an unforgettable photo of Rice seated on the senator's lap. Worse still, the photo was taken while the pair was aboard a yacht called *Monkey Business*. Hart's promising political career came to a sudden end.

In 1991 the Supreme Court nomination of Clarence Thomas was very nearly scrapped when he was accused of sexual harassment by a former employee, Anita Hill. The following year Senator Bob Packwood of Oregon, who was up for reelection, was accused of sexual harassment by a number of women. The press was persuaded to hold off on printing the accusations until after the election. Packwood won, but when the story came out he was forced to resign.

For President Clinton the situation was far worse. He risked more than being embarrassed in another Washington sex scandal. By the time the story broke, he was under investigation for having lied under oath about his relationship with Monica Lewinsky and having encouraged others to lie under oath in order to hide the relationship.

That was a potentially criminal offense, and possibly an impeachable offense as well.

The story of the former White House intern and the president immediately became the biggest story in the nation. At the time it broke the pope was visiting Fidel Castro's Cuba. It was a historic visit, and the news anchors of the three major networks had been sent to Havana to cover the event. But they all came rushing back to Washington to cover the spreading scandal. Monica Lewinsky had trumped Castro and the pope.

In January 1998 there were widespread predictions that the president would have to resign or he would be impeached, convicted, and removed from office. That had never happened to a United States president before.

2
The "Character" Issue

Bill Clinton's political career had always been dogged by rumors of sexual relations with women other than his wife. But the rumors had never really seemed to slow his rise to political power in his native Arkansas. The public appears willing to accept one standard of behavior from its governors; it demands a far higher standard of its presidents. Bill Clinton's presidential ambitions were very nearly derailed by a sex scandal.

In 1992, while Clinton was campaigning hard for the Democratic presidential nomination, a woman named Gennifer Flowers stepped forward to say that she had a twelve-year relationship with Clinton. She had tapes of telephone conversations with Clinton to back up her claim, and she had been given a state job in Arkansas, for which she was totally unqualified, while Clinton was governor.

Gennifer Flowers takes questions from the press after releasing her story to the *Star* tabloid.

Candidate Clinton strenuously denied the accusation. Flowers herself was not the best witness. A former lounge singer, she had sold her story to the tabloid press before going public.

Still, the Gennifer Flowers story sounded very credible and might have killed the chances of most candidates, but Clinton, an excellent and fierce political campaigner, fought on and managed to do well in the New Hampshire primary. He laid claim to the title of the "Comeback Kid." He then went on to win the Democratic nomination and the presidential election.

As his presidency began Clinton tried to put the stories of sexual misconduct behind him. Along with wife, Hillary, he sat down for an interview on the TV news program *60 Minutes*. The interview was broadcast on January 26, 1993, right after the Super Bowl and was one of the most watched news programs in U.S. history. Clinton admitted to having caused "pain" in his marriage—though he was not specific as to the reasons for the pain. When asked about the Flowers charges he insisted "the allegation is false," though he never specifically explained just what allegation he was denying.

This touches on another aspect of Bill Clinton's behavior—his tendency to play with words and say things that do not quite mean what they seem to mean. When confronted with questions about his youthful experiences with marijuana, he admitted that he had smoked it but said he "never inhaled." When asked about how he managed to avoid being drafted during the war in Vietnam, he said that he had simply "forgotten" about receiving a draft notice. In Arkansas his opponents had dubbed him "Slick Willie."

The *60 Minutes* interview was a triumph. With his wife, Hillary, loyally by his side, and not actually admitting anything, the president seemed to be saying that he was sorry for what he had done in the past and certainly wasn't going to do it anymore. The public may not have entirely believed him, but most people were eager to give the vigorous and charming new president the benefit of the doubt.

After very nearly losing his opportunity to become president, this intelligent and ambitious man would certainly not be foolish enough to risk everything he had worked for by carrying on with other women while in the White House? Would he? Not in the Washington of the 1990s where a politician's private life could very quickly become public property. Or so everyone thought.

Like all prominent political figures, Bill Clinton had his share of enemies—perhaps more than his share. Some politicians are hated because of their policies. This was not the source of Clinton's problems. He was a moderate, centrist Democrat; not a left-wing radical or even a traditional liberal. He was often accused by members of his own party of adopting Republican policies. Though his policies were opposed by many Republicans, that was politics as usual. The hatred that many on the political right felt toward Clinton was much more personal. In Bill Clinton and his alleged womanizing, pot smoking, draft dodging, and generally slippery morality, they saw a lack of basic "character." Clinton was the first president of the "Baby Boomer" era—that large generation born after World War II—an overindulged generation, born into an era of easy prosperity, that never knew the hardship and discipline of economic depression and total war. For some he became a living symbol of all that was wrong with America.

Many on the political right believed there was a "culture war" going on in America. It was a war between those who represented "traditional, conservative, American values," and those like Bill Clinton who were destroying these values. The depth of such feelings is hard to overstate.

Clinton's opponents had used the "character issue" against him when he first ran for president in 1992. It didn't work. They tried again when he ran for reelection in 1996. He won by an even bigger margin. But many could not shake the idea that no matter what the voters said Bill Clinton was not a legitimate president. He was morally unfit to lead the nation and he didn't deserve the job.

In the view of the more extreme Clinton haters, he was not only morally unfit, he was guilty of an astonishing number of crimes, including protecting drug smuggling and murder. The favorite Clinton "murder victim" was Vincent Foster, a longtime Arkansas associate and friend of the Clintons, who had come to Washington with them to work as a deputy White House counsel and the president's personal lawyer. On the afternoon of July 20, 1993, Foster ate lunch at his White House office, then drove twenty minutes to the generally deserted Fort Marcy Park in Virginia, and shot himself. All the evidence pointed to suicide. Foster had been under a great deal of personal pressure that he apparently could not handle.

For the extreme Clinton haters a suicide by a close Clinton associate was too innocent and tame an explanation. They insisted that Foster had been murdered because he "knew too much" about other Clinton scandals.

A vast conspiracy of drug running and murder involving the president was the theme of a video called *The Clinton Chronicles*, which was marketed by televangelist Jerry Falwell. Over 150,000 copies of this lurid film were sold.

While tales of drug running and murder provided excitement for Clinton's most rabid enemies, they pursued more mundane scandals as well. One of the most promising—from their point of view—centered on a woman named Paula Jones.

Jones had been an Arkansas state employee in 1991. She said that she had been working at the registration desk at a conference where then-Governor Clinton was supposed to speak. Later she said a state trooper came by with a message from the governor that he wanted to meet her in his hotel room. She went with the trooper. When she went into the room she said the governor made indecent advances to her, which she rejected.

In February 1994, Jones told her story to the media in a press conference sponsored by the Conservative Political Action Conference. It didn't make much of an impact at first. The president said he couldn't recall having even met Paula Jones. The fact that the story was being promoted by Clinton's sworn enemies also made it seem less credible.

Those in the Jones camp persisted. They brought a sexual harassment civil suit against Bill Clinton. The suit itself was on shaky legal ground, and even if it ever got to trial, the chances that Paula Jones would actually win were slight, because it would come down to her word against his. However, the potential for embarrassing the president was enormous. One of the things that the Jones lawyers would seek to prove was that Bill Clinton had a "pattern" of improper behavior toward women. That would give the lawyers a chance to question other women who had brought accusations against

REPUBLICAN
NATIONAL

The Reverend Jerry Falwell gives the
benediction at the Republican National
Convention in August 1996.

Clinton, or whose names had in one way or another been linked with him in the past.

Clinton's lawyers tried to block the case. They argued that while a president is not above the law, a sitting president should not be subjected to civil suits because preparing for them would be time consuming and distract him from his duties. He should be subject to a lawsuit only after he left office. On May 28, 1997, the Supreme Court in a surprising 9–0 ruling rejected the arguments of the president's lawyers and ruled the Paula Jones case could continue. Her lawyers could start taking depositions from witnesses under oath. Suddenly the Jones case looked more credible and threatening.

Still the president's problems did not appear critical. With the large number of legal options open to his lawyers, there was an excellent chance that the case would not actually come to trial before he left office, and it might not come to trial at all. The president's lawyers tried to settle the case out of court. In addition to money, Paula Jones's lawyers were also demanding a public apology from Bill Clinton. That would be an admission of guilt, and the president adamantly refused to make such an admission. But some compromise might be worked out. That is the sort of thing that happens in civil cases all the time. And since the legal grounds for bringing the case were shaky, it could still be dismissed. (In fact, on April 1, 1998, that is exactly what happened. But by that time the damage had been done).

Most of all the president's defenders were confident that the public didn't really care very much about something that was supposed to have happened before Clinton became president. People knew they had not elected a saint. The economy was strong, and the president's popularity was on the rise. The slogan was: The country cares more about the Dow Jones than Paula Jones.

A potentially more serious problem was Independent Counsel Kenneth Starr. The Office of the Independent Counsel (sometimes popularly called special prosecutor) had been established in the 1970s as a result of the Watergate scandal that brought down the Nixon administration. Before that, charges of wrongdoing by members of an administration were investigated by the Justice Department. During Watergate, however, some Nixon loyalists in the Justice Department themselves became part of the cover-up. A law was passed calling for the appointment of a prosecutor who was totally independent of the administration and who was given broad powers to investigate and, if necessary, prosecute cases of wrongdoing within an administration.

Since the law was passed, independent counsels had been appointed to investigate cabinet officers and others, up to and including President Ronald Reagan. Critics of the Office of the Independent Counsel complained that the prosecutor had too much power, which could easily be abused by a prosecutor who was following his own personal or political agenda.

Early in Bill Clinton's first term there were many reports that while governor of Arkansas he and his wife had been involved in some shady and possibly illegal financial transactions in connection with a land development scheme called Whitewater. An independent counsel named Robert Fiske was appointed to investigate Whitewater, but the Republicans in Congress didn't think he was aggressive enough. So in August 1994 a new independent counsel was appointed to take over the investigation. His name was Kenneth Starr, a former solicitor general and federal appeals court justice. Starr was a legal giant, with a fine reputation. He was also a staunch conservative Republican. Clinton supporters cried foul and said that Starr was on a crusade to "get" Bill Clinton no matter what.

By early 1996, Starr's office had won some impressive legal victories. Susan and Jim McDougal, who had been partners with the Clintons in the Whitewater deal, and Jim Guy Tucker, the sitting governor of Arkansas, had all been convicted of Whitewater-related crimes.

After that the investigation stalled without bringing prosecutors one step closer to the first family. In early 1997, Starr said he was going to resign to become dean of Pepperdine Law School in Malibu, California. That announcement raised a storm of protest and ridicule from editorial writers and others, and Starr reversed himself and stayed on.

The Office of the Independent Counsel extended its investigations far beyond Whitewater, into other allegations of wrongdoing by the Clintons. But by the end of 1997 all the investigations seemed stuck, and the work of Starr's office appeared to be winding down.

Up to that point there was no link between the many matters that the independent counsel was looking at and the Paula Jones case.

That critical link was provided by Linda Tripp.

3

Tapes

Linda Tripp was one of the army of civil servants who keep the government running no matter which administration is in office. The divorced wife of a retired army officer and mother of two, she had come to Washington during the administration of George Bush, who she came to revere. She worked in the White House as a secretary.

After Bush was defeated by Clinton, Tripp stayed on at the White House, though she came to detest the "Clintonites" who had taken over. She regarded them as arrogant, careless, disorganized, and of questionable morality. But as a career civil servant it was not necessary that she agree with or even like members of a new administration. It was only necessary that she do her job, and at this she was apparently very efficient.

Tripp seemed to have an uncanny knack for being on the spot when things happened. Her desk was right outside the office of presidential lawyer Vincent Foster. When Foster left his office at about one o'clock on July 20, 1993, he told Tripp, "I'll be back." He never came back. Foster drove to Fort Marcy Park in Virginia and shot himself. Linda Tripp may have been the last person to see him. When she arrived at work the next morning, she was appalled at the chaotic way in which the material in Foster's office was being handled by investigators, and she was not shy about making her disapproval known.

One of the people who Tripp had become friendly with in the White House was a volunteer worker from Virginia, Kathleen Willey. Willey was to figure prominently in the allegations of sexual misconduct that were to swirl around Bill Clinton. Willey claimed that on November 29, 1993, she had a private meeting with the president in the Oval Office. During the meeting she said that the president groped her and had made highly indecent sexual advances. She rejected him and walked quickly out of the office. The first person that the disheveled and flustered Willey met and talked to upon leaving the Oval Office was Linda Tripp.

Tripp was also quite friendly with FBI agent Gary Aldrich, who had worked in the White House and after he retired wrote *Unlimited Access*, a book that was supposed to be an insider's exposé of goings-on in the White House. The book was very popular with Clinton haters and denounced as a wildly inaccurate bundle of rumor and gossip by the president's supporters.

Linda Tripp, who was called to testify
about Whitewater in 1996

In 1995, Linda Tripp lost her job in the office of the White House counsel. The following year she was able to land a better-paying job at the Pentagon. Such bureaucratic shuffling is very common in Washington, but Tripp still resented the move. At the Pentagon she met, and befriended, another recent White House exile, former intern Monica Lewinsky.

The two women could not have been more different. Tripp was nearly twice Lewinsky's age. Tripp had spent much of her life in a military setting. Lewinsky had grown up in a million-dollar house in Beverly Hills, California. She was the precocious, overindulged, and rather spoiled child of a wealthy California doctor and his sometime writer wife. The couple had divorced when Monica was fourteen. She got her White House job as an unpaid summer intern, a plum job for rich young people, through the influence of an old family friend, who had been a major Clinton contributor. After her internship was over she got a low-level staff job at the White House.[1]

Lewinsky had numerous sexual affairs with men—some of them married. And she had no hesitation about talking freely about them. She was, in short, very much the sort of "Clintonite" that Linda Tripp so disliked.

Yet the two became friends, and very quickly Lewinsky began to relate an amazing and sensational story. She said that beginning late in 1995 she had an ongoing sexual relationship with President Clinton.

In April 1996, Lewinsky was shuffled out of her White House job by Evelyn Lieberman, deputy chief of staff, for spending too much time hanging around receptions and ceremonies, anyplace the president might appear. She was reassigned to the Pentagon, a move she protested vigorously. But the relationship continued, though as time went on the president paid less and less attention to her, Lewinsky complained. She said that the president had promised to bring her back to a White House job after the 1996 election, but that had not happened and she was disappointed and angry.

Linda Tripp was astonished by what she was being told. Lewinsky provided too many authentic-sounding details for her story to be dismissed as the fantasy of a starstruck young woman. Tripp, whose own children were about Monica Lewinsky's age, was genuinely appalled by Lewinsky's account of presidential behavior. It confirmed everything she already believed about Bill Clinton. She was also a bit frightened by the information because she knew that if the story could be proved true, it had the potential of doing enormous damage to the president. What her young friend was telling her was so potentially explosive that Tripp felt she could not handle it without help. So on September 18, 1997, she called Lucianne Goldberg.

Goldberg, a literary agent, Republican activist, self-confessed Clinton hater, and enthusiastic gossip and troublemaker, was one of the more colorful characters in this entire affair. Back in 1972, Goldberg was paid by Richard Nixon's campaign committee to pose as a member of the press and spy on the campaign of Nixon's Democratic challenger, George McGovern. She went on to write sexy novels about misbehaving politicians and then as an agent to promote conservative books, usually with a scandalous or sensationalist twist. Goldberg had tried to sell a book by an Arkansas woman who said she had a long-term affair with Clinton. But the woman insisted on presenting the tale as a novel, so the idea was never taken seriously. Goldberg was also on a paid retainer from the tabloid *New York Post* to supply items for their gossip columnists.

Tripp and Goldberg were not strangers to each other. Back in the spring of 1996, just after she left her job at the White House, Linda Tripp had an idea about writing a book on the Clinton presidency patterned after Aldrich's highly profitable *Unlimited Access*. A friend gave her Goldberg's name. The agent loved the idea and spent a lot of time trying to develop it. She came up with the title *Behind Closed Doors: What I Saw at the Clinton White House*. But in the end Linda Tripp got nervous. Even though she intended to write under a pseudonym, she was afraid that she would be found out and she would lose her job, and her reputation would be destroyed by Clinton loyalists. She backed out of the deal. Goldberg felt betrayed, and the two women hadn't spoken for months.[2]

But when it came to something really sensational Lucianne Goldberg was not one to hold a grudge—and what Linda Tripp was telling her about her young friend was truly sensational. *Newsweek* reporter Michael Isikoff concluded: "It was September 18, 1997, and for all intents and purposes, the plot that would threaten Bill Clinton's presidency was hatched that night."[3]

The problem was that Linda Tripp didn't have proof of anything. Though Monica Lewinsky was clearly angry about being ignored, she was not going to go public with her story. She would not betray the president. As it stood, all Linda Tripp had was titillating gossip about Bill Clinton, and there was plenty of that around already.

Goldberg told her that what she needed was tapes—she had to tape Lewinsky's phone calls. Since the young woman called her friend incessantly—as often as ten times a day, and talked about her relationship with Clinton in very graphic detail, there would be plenty to tape. Tripp was at first hesitant about secretly taping conversations with someone who was supposed to be her friend. And she worried that this sort of taping might not be legal. (Taping phone conversations when only one party knows the call is being recorded is legal in most states, but not in the state of Maryland, where Tripp lived and where the phone calls were being taped). But she finally agreed that it was the only way she could get the evidence that she felt she needed.

Linda Tripp began taping her long, rambling conversations with Monica Lewinsky on October 3, 1997.

Since the president was no longer regularly answering Lewinsky's phone calls, she began to write him letters. Tripp suggested that these letters be sent to the White House by special messenger. She even suggested a messenger service. This particular service, it turned out, had once been owned by a relative of Lucianne Goldberg, and she was on friendly terms with the current owner. Goldberg had the owner save copies of all the delivery tickets from Monica Lewinsky at the Pentagon. What prosecutors call a "paper trail" between Lewinsky and the White House was being established—though she was not aware of it.

Tripp and Goldberg also discussed ways of "getting the story out." (Goldberg was actually taping some of the phone conversations she had with Tripp, though Tripp didn't know this.) They talked of selectively leaking some of the information to mainstream reporters, particularly Michael Isikoff who was already looking into the many rumors of the president's womanizing. They also considered going directly to the tabloids with the story. Unlike the mainstream press, tabloids would pay for such a story—and probably pay a lot. But if the story appeared first in the tabloids it probably would not be taken seriously. That is what happened to the Gennifer Flowers story back in 1992.[4]

Another approach was to get information into the hands of the lawyers for Paula Jones. Monica Lewinsky could then be questioned, under oath, as part of the Jones lawyers' attempt to establish a "pattern of behavior" for the president. In addition, Bill Clinton could be questioned about Monica Lewinsky. And he too would be under oath. Through Goldberg's network of conservative friends, the lawyers were given the details.

For the president the problem was becoming more dangerous by the day. But at this point he still didn't know it.

4

Sti ng

On the afternoon of December 5, 1997, the president's lawyer, Bob Bennett, received a new list of potential witnesses from Paula Jones's lawyers. One of the names on the list was Monica Lewinsky. The president assured his lawyers that there were no problems involving any women in the White House.

But the president knew that there were problems, and he was soon to discover just how serious these problems could be. The following morning Monica Lewinsky showed up at the White House with a collection of small gifts for the president. They had exchanged gifts like a tie, a book, or a T-shirt on several occasions over the past two years. This time Lewinsky was stopped at the guard gate outside the White House and told that the president had another visitor. She became "hysterical" and stormed away.

3026

MSL-DC-00000621

2 March 1997

Dear Mr. P—

I must admit it... I am a compulsive shopper! I saw this tie and thought it would look fabulous on you. I hope you like it.

All of my life, everyone has always said that I am a difficult person for whom to shop. and yet, you managed to choose two absolutely perfect presents! A little phrase (with only eight letters) like "thank you" simply cannot begin to express what I feel for what you have given me. Art & poetry are gifts to my soul!

I just love the hat pin. It is vibrant, unique. and a beautiful piece of art. My only hope is that I have a hat fit to adorn it (ahhh, I see another excuse to go shopping)! I know that I am bound to receive compliments on it.

3027

I have only read excerpts from "Leaves of Grass" before – never in its entirety or in such a beautifully bound edition. Like Shakespeare, Whitman's writings are so timeless. I find solace in works from the past that remain profound and somehow always poignant. Whitman is so rich that one must read him like one tastes a fine wine or good cigar — take it in, roll it in your mouth, and savor it!

I hope you know how very grateful I am for these gifts, especially your gift of friendship. I will treasure them all... always.

Monica

MSL-DC-00000622

This letter from Monica Lewinsky to President Clinton was entered into evidence in the Starr Report.

Lewinsky had been unhappy at the Pentagon, and she had reconciled herself to the fact that she wasn't going to get another job at the White House. She was now very disillusioned with Washington. Her mother had just moved to New York City, and Lewinsky thought that she might like to get a job there. One suggestion was that she could be given a job at the United Nations, but that didn't seem to be working out.

Monica Lewinsky had already asked Bill Clinton if he could help her. She had even suggested to Clinton that Vernon Jordan might be just the man to help her get the sort of nongovernmental job she was looking for.

Jordan was a well-known Washington figure. The media regularly referred to him as a "super-lawyer." He didn't go into court and try cases, but he had a great deal of influence. He sat on the boards of a number of large corporations, and he seemed to know everybody. He was a longtime close friend of the president, and a lot of his influence was based on his willingness to do favors for his powerful friends.

When Lewinsky had her blowup outside of the White House, the president called her both to complain about her throwing a very public tantrum and to soothe her. He said he would talk to Jordan about the job. A week later she had lunch with Jordan, who now sounded much more encouraging and actively engaged in trying to find her a New York job.

The Paula Jones lawyers were getting more persistent in asking for information about Lewinsky. They wanted the president to turn over all communications with her. The president called her again, and for the first time told her that she might become ensnared in the Paula Jones case. Immediately after that call Lewinsky called Tripp, who recorded the conversation.

On the afternoon of December 19, a process server came to Monica Lewinsky's office at the Pentagon and handed her a subpoena. She was to appear to give a sworn deposition in the Jones case on January 23. She was also ordered to turn over all

Vernon Jordan is an old friend and golfing partner of President Clinton, as well as an important political ally.

This is the employee photograph of Monica Lewinsky from the Department of Defense, where she worked. It is an oft-seen image as it was the only one available until journalists caught up with her as the scandal unfolded.

correspondence with the president and every gift and present that he had ever given her. Though such an order could not have been completely unexpected, Lewinsky was stunned. She immediately called Vernon Jordan, who arranged for her to get a criminal lawyer.

In conversations with Tripp, Lewinsky said that she was going to deny everything because they couldn't prove anything. Tripp had also been subpoenaed to give a deposition to the Jones lawyers about Kathleen Willey. Lewinsky said that she could also deny everything. Tripp said she would not lie under oath, but would do everything she could to avoid talking to the lawyers. Time and again Lewinsky wondered out loud about who was "ratting her out"—telling Paula Jones's lawyers about her relationship with Bill Clinton. It never seems to have occurred to her that the person she was talking to, Linda Tripp, was the one. Tripp was an obvious suspect, but not the only one. Monica Lewinsky had already told a lot of people about the president.[1]

On December 28, Lewinsky was invited to the White House and met privately with the president. He gave her some small gifts, but then wondered out loud if it was a good idea for her to keep any of the gifts he had given her at her home. Later that day Lewinsky got a call from Betty Currie, the president's private secretary. Lewinsky and Currie had always been on very friendly terms. Just exactly what was said in this conversation is in dispute. Lewinsky recalled Betty Currie said, "The president said you have something to give me." Currie recalled that it was Lewinsky who asked her to come by and pick up the gifts. In any event Lewinsky packed up most, but not all, of the gifts the president had given her over the previous two years and turned them over to Currie, who came by her apartment.

By the time 1998 began, the worst of the crisis for Monica Lewinsky seemed to have passed. Her new lawyer had arranged for her to submit a sworn affidavit to the Jones lawyers, rather than appearing in person to be questioned. In the document she denied any sexual relationship with the president. Vernon Jordan had arranged for her to get a job with the public-relations department of the Revlon Corporation in New York. It was a plum job for someone with no previous experience, but Lewinsky still complained that the $40,000 a year salary was too low.

What Lewinsky didn't know, and what the president and his lawyers didn't know or even suspect, was that Monica Lewinsky's story was soon to become the property of Independent Counsel Kenneth Starr. It is still unclear exactly whose idea it was to tell Starr's office about Monica Lewinsky. It may have been Linda Tripp herself, though there are plenty of other possible suspects.[2]

Investigating a president's relationship with a White House staffer is a long way from investigating an Arkansas land deal. The independent counsel had sweeping powers, but not broad enough to investigate the president's personal conduct— which was not illegal. However, if the independent counsel had reason to suspect that the president had lied in sworn statements given to Paula Jones's lawyers and if he had encouraged Monica Lewinsky to lie in her affidavit, and to hide or destroy evi-

Throughout the year-long unfolding
of the Lewinsky affair, Betty
Currie held the sympathy of the
nation as someone who needed to
balance her personal integrity with
her loyalty to the president.

dence, like the gifts, and if he had helped to get her a job in order to keep her quiet—that was illegal and could be investigated.

On January 12, lawyers from Starr's office visited Linda Tripp for the first time. She knew they were coming and told them all about Monica Lewinsky, the president, Vernon Jordan, and Lewinsky's attempts to get her (Tripp) to lie under oath. She did not tell them about literary agent Lucianne Goldberg and her previous attempts to sell a book critical of the Clinton White House.

Tripp also said that she had an appointment to meet Lewinsky for lunch on the following day, and she had discussed with her own lawyer the possibility of "wearing a wire," using a concealed recording device so she could tape Lewinsky's conversation. She said she was worried about all the previously taped phone conversations because they might have been illegally obtained. However, one-party taping was legal in Virginia, and that was where the lunch was to take place.

Starr's prosecutors were horrified. They insisted that if any taping was going to be done it would be under their supervision. Linda Tripp said that would be fine, but the "sting" had to be organized in the next few hours. It was a mid-level prosecutor in Starr's office who made the fateful decision to go ahead with the operation.[3]

Tripp had made a date to meet Lewinsky at 2:45 P.M. at the Ritz-Carlton Hotel at the Pentagon City mall in Virginia. She arrived early and went to room 909. It was filled with FBI agents. One microphone attached to a microcasette recorder was strapped to her thigh. A small radio transmitter was clipped to the inside of her blouse. It was supposed to broadcast the conversation directly back to agents in room 908. But the transmitter didn't work, and that caused a panic among Starr's prosecutors because they didn't know what was going on. A couple of FBI agents were dispatched to sit at the next table to see if they could overhear the conversation. They couldn't.

The cassette recorder, however, was working just fine. The two women talked for nearly four hours. It was a rambling conversation, during which Lewinsky said many things that sounded incriminating. She even sounded as if she was trying to bribe Tripp to testify falsely. And it was all on tape.

After listening to the recording, it took Starr's office a couple of days to get legal clearance to take the next step. Tripp had arranged to meet Lewinsky in the food court at the Pentagon City mall on January 16. Tripp said she had a new lawyer and might be ready to sign an affidavit in the Jones case. They had things to discuss.

Linda Tripp arrived at 12:45. Monica Lewinsky was waiting for her at the foot of the escalator. As she stepped forward to greet her friend, Tripp made a swift motion with her hand, and two FBI agents stepped up and flashed their badges.

Lewinsky was frightened and completely bewildered. At first she had no idea what was happening—or why.

She had been stung.

5 "You Could Go to Jail . . ."

What actually took place during the next few hours is a subject that was to be hotly debated over the next year. It touched on one of the basic concerns of the entire impeachment saga.

Monica Lewinsky was to insist that she was detained, threatened, and bullied by FBI agents and prosecutors who were trying to get her not merely to confess but also to help gather additional evidence that would incriminate the president.

Investigators for Kenneth Starr's office responded by saying that they did nothing illegal, or indeed unusual. That the tactics they employed that day were standard procedure for prosecutors in criminal investigations.

The defense offered by the Office of the Independent Counsel was technically correct. What they did was standard prosecutorial procedure in many criminal cases. However, there was a deeper question. Monica Lewinsky was not an organized crime kingpin or an international spy. She was believed to be the president's sometime girlfriend. Lying under oath, even in a civil case, and encouraging others to lie or hide evidence, are criminal offenses. They are particularly serious for a president, who is sworn to uphold the nation's laws. But what was being lied about here was not burglary, as in Watergate, or any other obviously criminal offense. It was the president's private behavior. While most people might disapprove of his behavior, even be shocked by it, the behavior was not criminal and it did not directly affect the governing of the nation, so long as it remained private.

Was the perfectly legal but heavy-handed treatment of Monica Lewinsky really necessary? Or was Independent Counsel Kenneth Starr being too zealous in his attempt to "get something" on President Bill Clinton?

Lewinsky and Tripp were taken upstairs to a hotel suite where prosecutors told Lewinsky that they had a tape recording of her saying that she was going to lie under oath. They showed her pictures of her lunch with Tripp. She was told that she could be charged with a number of federal crimes, including perjury and obstruction of justice. These were serious crimes, they said, and she could go to jail for twenty-seven years.

Tripp said, "This is the best thing for you." Monica Lewinsky now realized what had happened, and she began to cry hysterically. Tripp was taken

Kenneth Starr was determined to follow
what began as the Whitewater investigation
all the way to the end.

out of the room, but it was still over an hour before Lewinsky was able to calm down enough to talk rationally. Even then the conversation was punctuated with bouts of sobbing and periods where she stared off into space and said nothing.

Prosecutors told Lewinsky they wanted her to cooperate with them, and if she did, that would influence whether or not she would be indicted. Cooperation meant being wired like Linda Tripp had been or taping phone calls. In legal slang they were trying to "flip" Lewinsky, turn her from a potential target of the investigation to sort of a double agent who was gathering evidence against others. They didn't tell her whose conversation they wanted to secretly record, but an obvious target would have been the president's personal secretary, Betty Currie.

Lewinsky was too distraught to agree to anything, or to turn anything down. After a couple of hours she asked if she could call her lawyer. She was completely within her rights to call her lawyer, but prosecutors didn't want her to because this was the lawyer who had been picked for her by Vernon Jordan—one of the targets of the investigation. They tried to discourage her from calling the lawyer.

Lewinsky didn't call her lawyer, but she didn't agree to cooperate either. After several more hours she asked if she could call her mother. Lewinsky recalled that the prosecutor said to her, "You're twenty-four years old, you're smart, you don't need to call your mommy." The prosecutor recalled that he said "mother" not "mommy."[1]

Whatever the word, Lewinsky did call her mother, Marcia Lewis, and then everybody had to wait until she arrived.

Prosecutors were in a hurry and getting very nervous. They faced two problems. First, bits and pieces of the Lewinsky story, including the content of a couple of the tapes, were already known to a few reporters. It was only a matter of time, and probably not very much time, until the whole thing came out in the media. At that point everyone who was being investigated would become extremely careful about what they said to or about Monica Lewinsky. A chance to get information that could be vital to the investigation could be lost.

A second problem was that early the next day— in just a matter of hours—President Clinton was scheduled to be formally deposed by lawyers for Paula Jones. If he knew that Monica Lewinsky was in the hands of Kenneth Starr's staff and cooperating with them, perhaps contradicting her own sworn affidavit, it was certain to have an impact on his testimony.

Monica Lewinsky's mother, Marcia Lewis, didn't arrive until about ten o'clock. She certainly didn't want to rush into anything and said they would have to call Monica's father. The couple had been divorced for several years and Dr. Bernard Lewinsky lived in California, but he was still close to his daughter. On the phone Dr. Lewinsky didn't want his daughter to do anything until she talked to a lawyer. And he would find the lawyer. Fifteen minutes later a man named William Ginsberg called. He was basically a medical malpractice lawyer, with little experience in criminal matters. But he was an old family friend who had known Monica since she was a baby. He was going to fly in from California. Until then Monica Lewinsky wasn't going to do anything. That was another delay.

The next morning the president sat down to be deposed under oath by the Jones legal team. The deposition was being recorded on videotape. Paula Jones was in the room, but the president never even looked at her. He had no idea that Lewinsky's detailed descriptions of their sexual relationship had been taped by Linda Tripp, that the tapes were in the hands of Jones's lawyers, and that Monica Lewinsky herself was already being questioned by Kenneth Starr's prosecutors.

The president was ready for some questions about Monica Lewinsky because her name had been on the potential witness list. But he was surprised by how detailed and relentless the questioning became. He dodged quite a number of questions and insisted that he "couldn't remember" or "didn't recall" the answers to others. But in the sworn answer to one question he appeared to be absolutely unequivocal. Bill Clinton said: "I have never had sexual relations with Monica Lewinsky. I've never had an affair with her." This was not a spontaneous, off-the-cuff remark. It was a well-rehearsed answer to a question that he knew was going to be asked.

That statement was shortly to get him in a lot of trouble. But he clearly was not aware of this when he made it. And when the deposition was over, both the president and his lawyers thought that it had gone pretty well.

Another scene of tension and high drama was being played out at the Washington offices of *Newsweek* magazine. The editors were trying to decide whether or not to run Michael Isikoff's Monica Lewinsky story. Isikoff had gathered a great deal of information. He had even listened to some of the Tripp/Lewinsky tapes. But he had never talked to Monica Lewinsky personally to get her version of events firsthand, or had a chance to judge her credibility. And he had never interviewed the president about Lewinsky. Despite all the detail and other circumstantial evidence, like the letters and packages that Lewinsky had sent to the White House by messenger, it was still possible that the young woman had simply made up the whole thing.

Since the story was obviously such an explosive one, the magazine's editors opted for caution and decided to hold off on publishing it until more checking could be done. Isikoff was shattered.[2]

Newsweek's decision to delay made absolutely no difference. In less than a day the bare bones of the Clinton/Lewinsky story were on the Internet. A few hours later the whole world knew.

America was about to enter one of the strangest, tawdriest, most tempestuous, and most depressing political years in its history.

6
Counter attack

According to *Time* magazine, President Bill Clinton was in high spirits after six hours of questioning by Paula Jones's lawyers. He thought the deposition had gone well for him. "Describing the mood Saturday night at the White House one person close to the president said: 'Everyone is going to sleep well tonight.'"[1]

If they did it was probably the last good night's sleep that the president and many of his supporters got for some time to come. By very early Sunday morning the Monica Lewinsky story began appearing on the Internet, and within days the trickle of revelations had become a flood.

At first the White House seemed stunned, and didn't quite know how to react. The president sat down with his secretary, Betty Currie, and asked a series of questions—or perhaps they were actually statements.

"I was never alone with Monica, right?

"Monica came on to me and I never touched her, right?

"Monica wanted to have sex with me and I cannot do that."

Was the president trying to influence the secretary to agree with his defense? Or was he just trying to "refresh" his own recollections, as Currie later testified.

Currie began calling Lewinsky, repeatedly. But on the advice of her new lawyer, William Ginsberg, Lewinsky wasn't returning these calls.

Ginsberg was already in the Office of the Independent Counsel trying to work out an immunity deal for his client.

Lewinsky was staying in the apartment still owned by her mother in the Watergate apartments, one of the best addresses in Washington. (The Watergate is forever associated with the scandal that forced president Richard Nixon to resign a quarter century earlier. This connection was not lost on the horde of reporters who had now been unleashed on to the story.) Lewinsky herself, who had once chatted so freely and frankly with Linda Tripp, and several others, was now completely silent. She talked only to her lawyer, her parents, and a few close, trusted, and discreet friends. She began to complain that it was almost like being a prisoner. Stuck in the apartment with little to do, she was bored and unhappy.

Photographers caught the occasional fleeting glimpse of Lewinsky with her lawyer, ducking in or out of a taxi. But news agencies began searching their archives and came up with a remarkable bit of videotape.

On November 6, 1996, Bill Clinton returned in triumph to the White House. He had just been comfortably reelected, the first Democrat since Franklin D. Roosevelt to win a second term. Just two years earlier the Republicans had taken control of both houses of Congress for the first time in forty years. Clinton was declared politically dead by his opponents and even by many of his friends. There was speculation that he wouldn't even run for a second term, and certainly he could never win.

But the "Comeback Kid" came back again, and the White House lawn was filled with cheering staff members. Many were lined up behind a rope barrier, and the president walked along the line shaking hands and hugging members of the jubilant crowd. At one point he passed a dark-haired young woman wearing a jaunty black beret, who was smiling and gazing up at him with what can only be described as an adoring look. The president stopped to give her a hug that was perhaps a little more affectionate and familiar than the hugs he had bestowed on others. The young woman in the beret was Monica Lewinsky. Over the next few months that clip was a regular feature of every TV news program in America.[2]

At first most congressional Republicans were content to stand quietly on the sidelines. They didn't want to step into the middle of what was sure to be an extremely messy Washington sex scandal. But not all Republicans felt that way. Representative Bob Barr of Georgia had been calling for Clinton's

This photograph from a television news clip is what convinced many heretofore unconvinced Americans that there was, indeed, a relationship between President Clinton and Monica Lewinsky.

impeachment months before he had ever heard of Monica Lewinsky. He was regarded as something of a right-wing fringe figure, even in his own party. Suddenly the idea of impeachment didn't seem quite so far-fetched. He was getting calls from reporters all over the country. "I look at this as a former prosecutor," said Barr. "When you see strong evidence, you don't just sit around. You move."

Democrats in Congress who had never been particularly close to the president anyway were reluctant to come out and publicly defend him. Even former White House staff members were uncharacteristically silent—or worse. George Stephanopoulos, once one of the president's closest advisers, wrote in *Newsweek*: "If true, the allegations about the president's relationship with Monica Lewinsky show that he failed to meet the standard of character that he set for himself, and shattered the promise he made to the public and the people around him. Right now I don't know whether to be angry, sad or both. But if the Lewinsky charges are valid, I know this: I'm livid. It's a terrible waste of years of work by thousands of people with the support of millions more."[3]

The president's staunchest and most effective supporter, as always, turned out to be the first lady, Hillary Rodham Clinton. She had stood by her husband throughout the Gennifer Flowers episode, and she stepped up to defend him once again. On television she spoke of the president as being the victim of a "vast right-wing conspiracy."

She was never entirely specific about the nature or extent of this conspiracy, but there were some obvious suspects.

Monica Lewinsky could not be attacked publicly. If she became angry at the president, there was no telling what she might say to Kenneth Starr. Even Linda Tripp had to be handled with care.

Lucianne Goldberg was another matter. Information about her background, including her career as a spy for Richard Nixon, was immediately faxed to every news organization in Washington. Goldberg was certainly a conspirator, but she was far too insignificant a figure to be a credible candidate for organizer of a "vast" conspiracy of any sort.

A more obvious and interesting possibility was Richard Mellon Scaife, a secretive Pittsburgh billionaire. Scaife, one of the heirs to the great Mellon fortune, had been a generous supporter of a variety of conservative causes. He had developed an intense hatred for Bill Clinton, and as early as 1993 was boasting that he would "get" Clinton. Scaife had come to believe, among other things, that Clinton had been responsible for the murder of Vincent Foster and others. "There must be sixty people [associated with Clinton] who have died mysteriously," he told an interviewer in the fall of 1998. Scaife gave substantial financial backing to some journalists who promoted these conspiracy theories. Scaife gave millions to the right-wing magazine *The American Spectator* for "The Arkansas Project," a largely unsuccessful attempt to dig up damaging information on the careers and lives of Bill and Hillary Clinton during their Arkansas days.[4]

Scaife also gave money to legal foundations that helped to pursue the Paula Jones lawsuit. He gave millions to Pepperdine University, which at one point had offered Kenneth Starr a lucrative faculty position. Officers of Scaife-supported foundations began appearing regularly on television to denounce Clinton. His huge fortune gave Richard Mellon Scaife a lot of influence, and he used it.

The "vast right-wing conspiracy" theory, however, did not gain wide acceptance, particularly since some of the most damaging information and scathing criticism appeared in publications like *The Washington Post* and *The New York Times*, which are generally considered to be on the liberal side of the political spectrum.

At the time the Lewinsky scandal broke, President Clinton was at the height of his popularity. The nation was prosperous and at peace. But as soon as the scandal hit, his popularity began dropping. Though the American people in general may have liked Bill Clinton personally, and as a president, they had serious doubts about his honesty and integrity. He had never really lost his reputation as a "womanizer" or as "Slick Willie." After Lewinsky, public distrust deepened. Private polls taken by the president indicated that he was in serious trouble, and that if all the allegations against him proved to be true, the public might actually support his being removed from office.

The president tried to avoid answering reporters' questions about the growing scandal. But when one reporter asked him if he would ever consider resigning from office, Clinton emphatically said, "Never!" Even those reporters who rarely believed anything Clinton said believed that statement.

At first the Clinton strategy was to try to say as little as possible about the Lewinsky matter. But that wasn't working too well. The more he refused to say anything, the more people wondered what he was hiding. An innocent man, they reasoned, would say he was innocent. Some of the president's advisers told him that he should give a statement that would leave no doubt in anybody's mind about what had or had not happened.

On the evening of January 27, 1998, the president was scheduled to deliver his State of the Union message, before both houses of Congress and a television audience of millions. In a normal year the State of the Union message is the most important single speech a president gives. He uses the address to highlight the accomplishments of his administration and outline his plans for the year to come.

In order to keep his State of the Union message uncluttered with talk of scandal, the president decided to make a statement on January 26, the day before the State of the Union message. It was an interesting choice of dates because it was also the sixth anniversary of Bill and Hillary Clinton's memorable *60 Minutes* interview in which he had acknowledged giving "pain" to his family and at least implying that nothing of that sort would ever happen again.

He stood behind a podium in the beautiful and historic Roosevelt Room of the White House, looked directly into the cameras, waggled his finger, and said, "I want you to listen to me. I'm going to say this again: I did not have sexual relations with that woman, Miss Lewinsky. I never told anyone to lie, not a single time. Never. These allegations are false."

The next evening he went over to Capitol Hill and delivered an enthusiastically upbeat State of the Union message. He did not once mention Monica

President Clinton, with Hillary at his side, absolutely denied having had an improper relationship with Monica Lewinsky.

Lewinsky or any of the other allegations that were swirling around him. The address was greeted with thunderous applause, even from many Republicans.

It was an absolutely bravura performance. Skeptical journalists, who had been predicting that the president would have to resign, were impressed.

Perhaps, somehow, Bill Clinton was going to get through all of this unscathed after all.

7

Testimony

After the outlines of the Monica Lewinsky story became public, the center of attention shifted to Washington's E. Barret Prettyman Courthouse. In a grand-jury room on the third floor, a group of twenty-three citizens had been convened by Independent Counsel Kenneth Starr to hear testimony about the actions of President Bill Clinton.

The purpose of a grand jury is widely misunderstood. A grand jury does not decide guilt or innocence. It is used by prosecutors to determine if there is enough evidence to indict someone for a crime. The grand jury is very much a prosecutor's tool. A common saying among lawyers is that a prosecutor can get a grand jury to indict a ham sandwich if he wants to.

Witnesses are called in to testify under oath and must answer questions from the prosecutor and members of the jury. The witness cannot be accompanied by a lawyer. If a witness refuses to testify, or testifies falsely, he or she is guilty of hindering prosecution or of perjury and can go to jail. The Fifth Amendment to the Constitution guarantees that no one is required to give testimony that might incriminate him or her. In many criminal cases the defendant does not even take the stand. But a prosecutor can give a witness immunity for grand-jury testimony. That means the witness cannot be prosecuted for anything that he or she says—but the witness is also required to testify fully and truthfully. It is a prosecutor's way of getting a reluctant witness who may be a minor figure in a case to give evidence that could be used against the main target of the investigation. Grand juries can sit for months and can hear evidence in a variety of related cases.

Unlike ordinary trials that are open to the public, grand-jury proceedings are closed, and are supposed to be secret. Disclosing grand-jury testimony is a serious offense.

Without any real hard news coming out of the grand jury, reporters prowled the corridors of the courthouse in order to see if they could find out who had been called before the grand jury that day. The identity of witnesses could give reporters some indication of what direction the investigation might be heading. Anyway, it was all the news they had.

Just across the street from the courthouse was a little stretch of concrete that came to be known as "Monica Beach."[1] That's where all the television crews and photographers were set up. Well-known witnesses had to run the gauntlet of lights and cameras while entering and leaving. Sometimes witnesses would say a few words to the assembled media, usually that they had answered all questions fully and truthfully. But that was about all.

While there was little hard news coming from the courthouse, there were some memorable and, ultimately, influential moments. There was a frightened-looking Betty Currie being hustled past the media crowd. There was Monica Lewinsky's mother, Marcia Lewis, emerging from her encounter with the grand jury, ashen-faced and apparently near collapse. Rumors circulated that she had become so overwrought during her testimony that she had to be excused.

Rightly or wrongly, images like these contributed to Kenneth Starr's growing reputation as a zealot who would do anything and hurt anybody to get the president.

Though she was a longtime Democratic activist and Clinton loyalist, who may well have provided cover for Clinton-Lewinsky meetings, Betty Currie was a warm-hearted person who was well liked in Washington, even by those who hated Clinton. Marcia Lewis was very close to her daughter, and it was quite reasonable to suspect she knew a great deal about her relationship with the president. During the phone conversations recorded by Linda Tripp, Lewinsky sometimes broke away to take a call from her mother. Yet Marcia Lewis was a mother who was being asked, indeed ordered, to testify against her own daughter. People felt sorry for her.

By contrast Tripp, who testified before the grand jury eight times, did not come across as a sympathetic character at all when she faced the cameras at

Monica Beach. After her final day of testimony, she came out and read a prepared statement in which she insisted that she was just an ordinary American who did what anyone else would have done when she secretly taped intimate phone conversations with someone who was supposed to be a close friend. A lot of people were insulted by the comment.

Most of the time was spent "waiting for Monica." Lewinsky's testimony was the key to any case that Starr might build. But would she testify? And if she did, how much was she willing to say?

Lewinsky's lawyer, William Ginsberg, began negotiating with the Office of the Independent Counsel almost immediately. He wanted immunity from prosecution if she testified. But she was still only willing to admit to her affair with Clinton. She continued to insist that no one had ever asked her to lie, and that she had not tried to persuade anyone else to lie. Negotiations stalled and then seemed to break down. Ginsberg accused Starr of trying to pressure and "squeeze" his client by subpoenaing her relatives and friends.

Ginsberg, the California malpractice lawyer and old Lewinsky family friend, transformed himself into one of the more curious figures in the story. He fell in love with his newfound celebrity. Suddenly he seemed to be on television all the time giving folksy, wide-ranging interviews and saying one thing one day and something very different the next. He began appearing at fashionable Washington parties, and when he dined out at a fancy restaurant with his famous client, which was frequently, the event became an item in the gossip columns.

He even encouraged Lewinsky to pose for a series of glamour photographs for the trendy magazine *Vanity Fair*. Ginsberg thought the photos would cheer her up. There was nothing even faintly suggestive about the pictures, but since Monica Lewinsky was at the center of a major political crisis in America, this sort of photo spread just made her look shallow and silly and contributed to the carnival-like atmosphere that was rapidly gathering around the scandal.[2]

Every tidbit, every rumor became front page, top-of-the-hour news every day and every night, week after week. *The New York Times*, *The Washington Post*, and the network news broadcasts were now regularly discussing subjects that just a few weeks earlier would have been taboo for them.

Cable news/talk shows like *Larry King Live* and *Rivera Live*, which a year earlier had been almost entirely devoted to discussion of the O. J. Simpson case, now switched to full-time nightly discussion of the Clinton/Lewinsky story. Often it was the very same revolving panel of "experts" who had made a career giving their opinions about the California celebrity murder who again appeared night after night. Clinton loyalists squared off against Clinton haters in televised shouting matches.

It wasn't very informative, but it was popular. Larry King quipped that if he had scheduled an interview with God and Monica Lewinsky became available, he would have to reschedule God.

While negotiating with Lewinsky's lawyer, the Office of the Independent Counsel was busy building its case without her testimony. Starr's prosecutors subpoenaed White House visitor and phone logs. These indicated that Lewinsky had visited the White House at least thirty-seven times in the twenty months after she left her job there. And there were numerous phone calls.

All of this information, which had been given to the grand jury was supposed to be secret, but it appeared in the newspapers. Each side accused the other of leaking the information.

When some close associates of the president, and members of the secret service, which protects the president, were subpoenaed, the White House countered by claiming "executive privilege." The law grants certain privileges against testifying—spouses do not have to testify against each other, lawyers do not have to give testimony against their clients, and so forth. During the Watergate scandal President Richard Nixon's lawyers asserted that certain key members of the executive branch did not have to testify against the chief executive—the president. The courts did not uphold that claim in the 1970s, and they were no more impressed by it when President Clinton's lawyers raised it. Such legal challenges delayed the Starr investigation somewhat but did not derail it. White House lawyers lost a string of court battles with the Office of the Independent Counsel.

The battle was being waged on two fronts, the legal side and public side. While the president was losing the legal side, he was winning the fight for public support.

Immediately after the scandal broke, polls showed a sharp drop in the president's popularity.

After his upbeat State of the Union message his popularity was on the rise again. Within two months after the American public first heard of Monica Lewinsky, Bill Clinton was more popular than he had ever been—indeed his approval ratings were higher than those of any other president since polling of that type began.

As the president traveled around the country making speeches—though never mentioning the scandal—he was greeted by small groups of protesters demanding his resignation or impeachment. These were overshadowed by much larger crowds of Clinton supporters eager to see and cheer the president. While the popularity of the president grew, public attitudes toward his nemesis Kenneth Starr became increasingly negative.

What Clinton's opponents found most frustrating, nearly maddening, was that even though some of the president's supporters thought he was lying about his relationship with Monica Lewinsky they just didn't care that much.

The president won some legal victories as well. In Arkansas on April 1, Judge Susan Webber Wright, who was presiding over the Paula Jones lawsuit threw out the whole case. Thus the case that had been the basis of Starr's investigation of the president and Monica Lewinsky had been dismissed. Legally this didn't have any effect on the investigations, but it gave the president's defenders a powerful new public-relations weapon. The president, who was in Africa at the time, was filmed smoking a cigar and beating a small drum after hearing the news. The sight of Bill Clinton celebrating drove his opponents into a frenzy.

One of those who appeared most frequently on television to denounce the president's moral failings was former Reagan and Bush administration official and author of the best-selling *The Book of Virtues*, William J. Bennett. (Also, ironically, the brother of President Clinton's chief lawyer, Bob Bennett.) In the late summer of 1998, Bennett poured out his frustrations and anger in a book called *The Death of Outrage: Bill Clinton and the Assault on American Ideals*.

Bennett tried to end on a hopeful note:

> *Here is my hope. The American citizens know better—and they will demonstrate that indeed they do know better. Americans will realize that they are being played for fools by the president and his defenders. They will declare, with confidence, that a lie is a lie, an oath is an oath, corruption is corruption. And truth matters.*

Those who thought like Bennett fervently hoped that once all the facts were laid out, and all the tawdry activities and evasions became known, then the American people would finally become outraged and Bill Clinton would be forced from office.

The conclusive evidence looked like it might at last become available. By June, Lewinsky replaced her lawyer, the old family friend William Ginsberg, with Jacob Stein and Plato Cacheris, two high-powered Washington insiders and seasoned deal makers. Within weeks the new lawyers had negotiated an agreement for full immunity with the Office of the Independent Counsel. Monica Lewinsky would testify.

In addition to agreeing to testify, Lewinsky turned over a number of items that the independent counsel had wanted. Among them was a dark blue dress that allegedly was stained with the president's semen. There had been rumors about the dress for months. On the phone tapes Linda Tripp had urged her friend not to destroy the dress and not to have it cleaned. Laboratory tests identified the president's DNA.

Early on the morning of July 28, Monica Lewinsky was rushed past the overflow media crowd gathered at Monica Beach in front of the federal courthouse. She took the private elevator up to the third floor and testified for over six hours. Under oath she admitted that she had a sexual relationship with President Bill Clinton at the White House between November 1995 and May 1997. Her testimony was emotional, graphic, and detailed. But in the end it contained very little the public had not already heard through leaks and rumors. And she did not say that the president had ever told her to lie under oath or had arranged for her to get a job in order to buy her silence.

Still, the president who had looked straight into the television cameras and told the American public that he never had sexual relations with "that woman" was in a serious bind.

The Office of the Independent Counsel had already served the president with a grand-jury subpoena in mid-July. That was an unprecedented act, and the White House might have been able to challenge it in court. The president and his lawyers decided not to, and after negotiations the president agreed to testify and the subpoena was withdrawn. More negotiations were needed to agree on circumstances under which the testimony would be given.

An ordinary citizen in Bill Clinton's position would almost certainly have invoked his constitutional right not to testify. But the president is not an ordinary citizen and "taking the Fifth" before a grand jury was considered to be political suicide. He had to testify. But how?

For a sitting president to actually go to the federal courthouse to be questioned by the grand jury was unthinkable to the White House. It was equally unthinkable to bring the entire grand jury to the White House to take the testimony. The compromise finally worked out was that the president was to give his testimony from the White House Map Room. It would be broadcast live via closed-circuit television to the grand jury back at the courthouse.

President Clinton had some advantages that an ordinary grand-jury witness does not have. His lawyer would be in the room with him, not on camera, but in easy consultation range. There were also dangers. Hackers might be able to break into the live feed and obtain pirate copies of the president's testimony. (That never happened, but the fear was real enough.) A videotape would automatically be made of the testimony, and while it would be secret like all grand-jury testimony, the Office of the Independent Counsel could, under some circumstances, release the tape to Congress. After that who knew what might happen?

President Clinton's grand-jury testimony in the Lewinsky matter was given on August 17. It lasted over four hours.

That evening the president went on nationwide television to admit to what he called an "improper relationship" with Monica Lewinsky. The statement was brief and carefully worded. He said that he had misled his wife and the American public. He said that he was "solely and completely responsible" for a critical lapse of judgment and personal failure. But he also insisted that he had not obstructed justice or tried to cover up the relationship by urging anyone to lie. He said even presidents have private lives and angrily demanded his privacy back. He said that the investigation had gone on too long, cost too much, and hurt too many people and it was now time to move on.

This was by no means the full confession and abject apology that many had expected and hoped for. Even some of the president's supporters were disappointed by the harsh tone and apparent lack of remorse. Over the next few weeks President Clinton made a series of more contrite statements to members of his staff and others. But he did not waver in his basic position that he had done nothing legally wrong, and committed no impeachable offense. It was clear that the struggle between the president and the prosecutor was not about to end anytime soon.

8 The Report and the Reaction

On September 9, 1998, Kenneth Starr's Office of the Independent Counsel dispatched two vans to the Capitol. Thirty-six sealed boxes containing two complete copies of the independent counsel's report and supporting evidence were turned over to Wilson Livingood, sergeant at arms of the House of Representatives.

In a covering letter addressed to Speaker of the House Newt Gingrich, Kenneth Starr wrote: "This referral is filed in conformity with the requirements of Title 28, United States Code, Section 595 (c) which provides that '[a]n Independent counsel shall advise the House of Representatives of any substantial and credible information which such independent counsel receives . . . that may constitute grounds for an impeachment.'"[1]

It had been widely known that Starr's staff had been working on a report to submit to Congress, but the speed with which it had been prepared and the secrecy under which it had been delivered took most Washington observers by complete surprise.

The report was long and highly detailed. It contained many extremely graphic accounts of the president's sexual encounters with Monica Lewinsky, taken from her testimony.

It listed eleven "acts that may constitute grounds for an impeachment." These included repeated acts of lying under oath or attempting to obstruct justice. The final act read: "There is substantial and credible information that President Clinton's actions since January 17, 1998, regarding his relationship with Monica Lewinsky have been inconsistent with the President's constitutional duty to faithfully execute the laws."[2]

The evidence was quite overwhelming. If there was any good news for the president in what came to be universally known as the "Starr Report" it was that it focused solely on Monica Lewinsky. There was no information at all about any of the other alleged presidential scandals, which Kenneth Starr had been investigating for years and at considerable cost.

What happened next was even more surprising. Two days later the House by an overwhelming vote of 363 to 63 voted to release the 445-page report to the public—uncensored. Within hours the entire Starr Report was available on the Internet. The next day it was printed in full in many major newspapers, and within weeks it was out in book form,

The Internet had it first, and thousands logged on to be the first to read the Starr Report.

both hardback and paperback. The Starr Report was briefly a best-seller.

There was more to come. All of Starr's evidence was turned over to the House Judiciary Committee. The committee then began releasing thousands of pages of grand-jury evidence. The most sensational release of all came on September 21 when the committee turned the tape of President Clinton's grand-jury testimony over to the media. Very few were going to take the time to read thousands of pages of testimony, but practically anybody could watch a few hours of televised testimony.

The White House had objected vigorously to the release of the tape, insisting that out-of-context clips could be used by Republicans in advertising for the elections coming up in just a few weeks. There had also been a series of rumors—no one is sure where they started—that during the session Clinton exploded in anger at the personal questions being asked and stormed out of the White House Map Room. Later Republicans were to wonder ruefully whether all of this had been part of a secret White House attempt to build up interest and expectations regarding the tape.

While the nation watched the president on tape testifying about sex, Bill Clinton himself was addressing the United Nations and New York University Law School. He was warmly greeted at both institutions. A word often used to describe the day was "surreal."

The testimony ran a little over four hours, and it was shown in its entirety or nearly so on all the major TV news outlets. What the public saw was a clever, agile, and thoroughly in control performance by the president. He did not storm out of the Map Room. On the contrary, he was generally polite, even contrite, and when he was combative he never really looked or sounded angry. "I'd give anything in the world not to have to admit what I've had to admit today," he said.

Though President Clinton had reportedly told associates that Monica Lewinsky was a "stalker," in his testimony he described her as "basically a good girl." His enemies, he insisted, were behind the attempts to expose his private life: "They just thought they would take a wrecking ball to me and see if they could do some damage."

He bobbed and weaved his way through a series of pointed questions, insisting that his previous testimony under oath was "legally accurate," though it may have been misleading. In order to avoid admitting that he had actually committed perjury, he split rhetorical hairs about the definition of "sex" or what "alone" really meant. The evasions were tortured and obvious, but somehow they did not appear sinister. Bill Clinton looked like a man defending himself, as best he could, from a humiliating inquisition into his sex life.

Many of the president's opponents had predicted that once he was seen on camera defending his deceit and evasions, people who had been inexplicably supporting him for so long would finally turn against him.

The opposite happened. Clinton's job approval rating jumped again, and more significantly, polls showed that there was now a serious backlash against Kenneth Starr, Republicans in Congress, and the House Judiciary Committee, which was considering whether to begin formal impeachment hearings.

A *New York Times* poll found that most Americans disapproved of the way all of the information was dumped on them, and they turned their annoyance against those who had been pushing the material out. Most said they disapproved of the way the House Judiciary Committee was handling the affair; three quarters did not think it was necessary to make the video public, and 43 percent said Congress should drop the whole Lewinsky matter, compared with only 27 percent who wanted impeachment hearings and 26 percent who wanted the president to be censured by Congress or given some other punishment short of impeachment. And Starr was further damaged when the White House pointed out that his voluminous report did not include Lewinsky's statement to the grand jury that "no one ever asked me to lie, and I was never promised a job for my silence."

It wasn't that the American people approved of Bill Clinton's behavior; they didn't, by a wide margin. Pollster John Zogby found that half the voters were ashamed that Clinton was president. But they apparently had concluded that what they wanted was an effective manager, not a moral role model. "The public isn't ready for impeachment, and any quick movement toward that will backfire," Zogby concluded.[3]

The House Republicans were not listening to such advice. On October 5, on a straight party-line vote, the House Judiciary Committee recommended holding a full impeachment inquiry. On October 8 the full House authorized an impeachment inquiry by a vote of 258 to 176. Thirty-one Democrats broke ranks to vote with the Republican majority.

But in politics it is often said that the only poll that really counts is the one that is held on election day. There was a national election coming up on November 3.

The Republicans controlled both houses of Congress, but by narrow margins. Early in the year they had high hopes of making major gains. History was with them. Traditionally the party that does not hold the presidency gains congressional seats during an off-year election. And then there was the Lewinsky scandal. Bill Clinton was not on the ballot, but the scandal had dominated the news all year. A lot of Democratic candidates had tried to distance themselves from the president, and Republicans had tried to make the election a referendum of Clinton's behavior.

The closer the election came, however, the less confident Republicans were of this strategy. Some Democrats, who had privately been saying that the president should resign in order to save the party, began to embrace him.

Early in the year, Republicans had hoped to gain as many as thirty seats in the House and five in the Senate. By election eve they were hoping for eight to ten new seats in the House and two or three in the Senate. That would have been in line with historical averages, and they could legitimately claim victory.

When the votes were counted, however, the overall balance in the Senate had not changed at all, and in the House the Republicans had actually lost five seats. That kind of loss in a midterm election for a party that did not control the White House had not happened since Franklin D. Roosevelt's first term in 1934.

If the 1998 congressional election was to be interpreted as a referendum on President Bill Clinton, then Bill Clinton was the clear winner.

The fallout was immediate. Speaker of the House Newt Gingrich, the Republican firebrand and strategist who had led his party to a historic congressional win in 1994, resigned his position, and actually resigned from Congress, though he had been reelected. Gingrich had always been a lightning rod, and he was the best-known Republican leader in the country.

The year had begun with predictions of Bill Clinton's resignation. It drew to a close with the resignation of one of his chief political opponents.

And the year wasn't over yet.

9

Impeachment

The November 1998 elections showed as clearly as anything could that the American public was in no mood to see President Bill Clinton removed from office.

Immediately after the election most experienced political observers believed that Congress would not try to remove the president; that some other method of showing disapproval, perhaps a vote of censure, would be crafted. For a time it seemed that even the president would have been willing to go along with such a compromise.

But once again in this tangled affair conventional wisdom turned out to be wrong. Politics usually involves compromise. This time in this battle the lines had been too sharply drawn, and the hatred on both sides was too deep to allow for any easy solution.

The U.S. Constitution provides Congress with a method for removing a president. But the Constitution does not provide a detailed road map. A president can be removed for "Treason, Bribery or other High Crimes and Misdemeanors." Treason and bribery are clear enough. But what are "High Crimes and Misdemeanors?" The Constitution is deliberately vague on this point. Does lying about a consensual sexual affair constitute an impeachable offense, particularly when the lawsuit in which the lies were originally told was later dismissed? This was the key question that Congress had to answer.

The first step in removing a president is taken in the House of Representatives. The House hears the charges and then votes on resolutions of impeachment. All the House needs is a simple majority to impeach. But that's only the beginning of the process. The articles of impeachment are then sent over to the Senate for a formal trial to remove the president.

The process isn't easy, and it's not supposed to be. Removing a president is the gravest act Congress can perform short of declaring war. The president is the only official elected by the entire country. Removing him would essentially mean overturning the decision of the American people. The preferred method of removing a president is to vote him out of office. President Clinton's term would end in two years, and the Constitution barred him from running for reelection again.

Only one American president had ever been impeached. That was Andrew Johnson in 1868. The Senate failed by one vote to convict him, and he served out his term. Johnson's impeachment came shortly after the Civil War, and the wounds of war were still raw. Johnson had never been elected, he was vice president at the time of Lincoln's assassination. He was an unelected and in a sense an accidental president.

Richard Nixon was never actually impeached. In July 1974 the House Judiciary Committee had voted to recommend three articles of impeachment to the full House. President Nixon resigned before a House vote was taken. If he had not resigned he almost certainly would have been impeached.

Impeachment has often been compared to grand-jury proceedings, where the House of Representatives decides if there is enough evidence to "indict" the president and send the case to the Senate for trial. The comparison can be misleading for there are fundamental differences. The House has to decide what an impeachable offense is, and then whether there is substantial evidence that the president committed such an offense. Grand-jury deliberations are secret, the arguments in the House are public—and in this case televised. Impeachment proceedings are intensely political, which is exactly what the framers of the Constitution intended they should be.

Those who opposed censure, or any other compromise solution, said they did so because there was no provision for censure or any other punishment for presidential misbehavior in the Constitution except impeachment and removal from office. They argued, successfully, to let the constitutional process play itself out.

The impeachment process started in the House Judiciary Committee, which was unfortunate for

When the possibility of censure was denied, minority leader Richard Gephardt led Democrats in a symbolic walkout in protest.

those who favored compromise. The committee was one of the most partisan in the House, split between conservative Republicans and liberal Democrats, with the Republicans in the majority. There were not many voices for compromise in that group.

Chairman of the committee was Representative Henry Hyde of Illinois, a portly, white-haired legislator in his seventies. His politics were impeccably conservative, but he was also considered an extremely intelligent, highly principled, and very fair man. He was one of the most respected members of the House and generally well liked, even by those who strongly disagreed with him.

Shortly after the committee hearings began, a story surfaced that Hyde had once had an affair that nearly broke up his marriage. Hyde brushed the incident off as a "youthful indiscretion." In fact, the affair had occurred when he was in his forties, not youthful, and went on for several years, hardly an indiscretion. It did break up the woman's marriage.

But it had all happened over thirty years ago, before Henry Hyde was even a congressman. He had reconciled with his wife, and was now a widower. The story had been known for a long time. Until the fall of 1998 and the impeachment hearings, newspapers wouldn't touch it. That had all changed. Everybody was fair game now.

In October, Larry Flynt, publisher of the sex magazine *Hustler* and a self-described "smut peddler," put a full-page ad in *The Washington Post* offering "up to one million dollars" to informants with proof of adulterous affairs with current members of Congress and high-ranking government officials.[1]

At first the offer looked like a cheap publicity stunt. But it bore fruit. One of those entrapped by Flynt's offer was Bill Clinton's harshest and most persistent critic, Representative Bob Barr. Barr, who had been married three times and was an outspoken foe of abortion, was accused of having paid for his second wife's abortion and of cheating on her with his current wife. Barr didn't exactly deny the charges but said that he had never committed perjury and would not discuss details of his personal life.

The atmosphere in Washington had become absolutely poisonous.

On November 5 the House Judiciary sent the president eighty-one questions about his actions. Republicans found his responses evasive and legalistic. For example, in one response the president questioned the definition of "alone." Clinton admitted that he had given misleading responses to the Jones lawyers but continued to insist that he had not crossed the legal line into perjury.

Even some Democrats found the president's responses completely unsatisfactory, and almost insulting.

The Republicans on the committee had already agreed to severely limit the length of the hearings. They wanted it all over and done with before the end of the year. If the hearings had dragged on, the newly elected Congress, in which Republicans held an even slimmer majority, would take over, and there was no way of telling how the vote would go then. During the committee deliberations the Republicans called only one witness, Independent Counsel Kenneth Starr himself. Starr testified for nearly twelve hours. He went over the findings of his office in great detail, and defended them vigorously but added no new information. He was then questioned by the president's lawyer, David Kendall. Once again the questions were familiar and so were the answers.

The president's Democratic defenders called a string of law professors and former Democratic congressmen. The aim was not to dispute the basic facts of the case but to focus in on narrow questions of whether the president had technically committed perjury, and whether his misdeeds rose to the level of an impeachable offense.

The debate in the Judiciary Committee was bitter and partisan and sometimes highly personal. The final vote to recommend impeachment to the full House was strictly along party lines.

By mid-December when the full House was scheduled to vote on impeachment, all attempts at

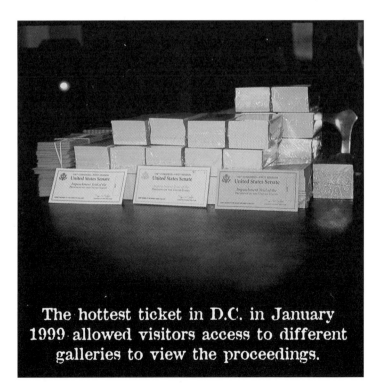

The hottest ticket in D.C. in January 1999 allowed visitors access to different galleries to view the proceedings.

forging a compromise—like a resolution of censure that would avoid actual impeachment—had collapsed. The House Republican leadership was absolutely convinced that William Jefferson Clinton must be impeached. House Republican leaders applied very heavy pressure to those moderate Republicans who were wavering and might vote against impeachment. This was a vote they did not intend to lose.

On the Democratic side, leaders were equally determined to maintain party discipline, in order to give the Republicans as narrow a victory as possible.

Before the impeachment hearings began President Clinton had always been referred to as just plain Bill. It was a simple and friendly name. Most Americans probably didn't even know the president had a middle name. Now, with a formal inquiry under way, he became William Jefferson Clinton. The use of the president's full legal name sounded very formal and ominous.

What just a few weeks earlier had seemed unthinkable was about to happen. The president was going to be impeached—the first time that had happened in 130 years. No living person had ever witnessed the impeachment of a U.S. president.

There was still one more surprise. Before the final debate began Congressman Bob Livingston of Louisiana, who had just been chosen to become the new Speaker of the House, replacing Newt Gingrich who had resigned, rose and announced to the entire membership and the television audience that he, too, had affairs with women other than his wife. He then said that he was going to resign the speakership and his seat in the House. He suggested that

President Clinton should follow his example and also resign.

The announcement was completely unexpected, and House members, particularly Republican members, were stunned. House Majority Whip Tom DeLay of Texas, who had really been leading the impeachment drive, had tears in his eyes. He called Livingston's actions noble and unselfish and also urged a presidential resignation.

What had happened was that Livingston had been caught in Larry Flynt's net. The evidence that Flynt had gathered was just about to be made public. The congressman beat him to it.

On Saturday, December 19 on a near party-line vote, the United States House of Representatives voted to approve two articles of impeachment of the president—one for perjury before the grand jury about his relationship with Lewinsky and a second for obstruction of justice in the Paula Jones lawsuit.

Almost immediately after the vote about one hundred Democratic congressmen, the president's most ardent supporters, were bused up Pennsylvania Avenue to the White House where they were greeted by Bill Clinton and members of the White House staff on the South Lawn. He thanked the congressmen for their support and they cheered lustily.

President Clinton had just become only the second president to be impeached, yet it looked as if he was celebrating.

10 Trial and the End

After the House vote to impeach, President Clinton should have felt that he had good reason to believe that he would not be convicted by the Senate and removed from office. In the House, Democratic party lines had held; there were only a handful of defections. The same had been true on the other side, only a handful of Republicans had voted against impeachment.

But the House could impeach by a simple majority. In the Senate it took a two-thirds vote to convict. While the Republicans were in the majority, they didn't have that large of a majority, and there were no signs of mass Democratic defections. Many Democrats, including some of the president's longtime allies in the Senate, had publicly expressed anger, disappointment, even disgust with the way the president had behaved. But not a single Democratic senator had announced that he or she would vote to remove the president, and most were firmly on record as opposing conviction.

Still, a few months earlier it had seemed impossible that the president would even be impeached; yet it had happened. While conventional wisdom in Washington was that the president would not be convicted, nothing in this entire affair had turned out the way Washington insiders had predicted, so there was still a bit of suspense.

The senatorial trial of an impeached president is an odd affair as outlined in the Constitution. The Chief Justice of the United States comes over to the senate chamber to preside over the trial. The case for the prosecution—to convict the president—is handled by a group of "managers," members chosen by the House to present the evidence. The president's defense is handled by lawyers that he has chosen. Unlike a defendant in an ordinary trial, the president does not sit in on the proceedings. He is supposed to be back at the White House doing the country's business.

Those are the basic rules. After that the Senate can do pretty much what it likes. It can decide how many witnesses each side can call, who they will be, or indeed if any witnesses at all will be called. It can decide whether the sessions will be held in public or behind closed doors. It can change the charges in the middle of the trial or simply decide not to vote.

Since there had been only one other trial of a president in U.S. history, there were few precedents to build on.

When the Constitution was written, the framers envisioned very different roles for the House and the Senate. Members of the House were elected from small districts for a two-year term. They were supposed to be closer to the people and able to reflect the popular will of the moment.

The Senate was designed as a "deliberative" body, one that acted more slowly and carefully. Senators were elected by an entire state; in fact, until 1913 when the Seventeenth Amendment was passed, senators had been chosen by state legislatures and not by direct election. They served six-year terms. The Senate was designed to be a body that would not be easily swept up in temporary political passions. It is a role that the Senate takes very seriously indeed.

The impeachment hearings in the House had not played well with the American public. People were angered and offended by what many regarded as an embarrassing display of trivial and partisan bickering.

Senators from both sides of the aisle were adamant that they wanted a proceeding that was fair, dignified, and brief. They were Republicans and Democrats, but more than anything else they were senators who had to protect the reputation of the institution.

The thirteen house managers, led by Representative Henry Hyde, had been appointed from among the Republican members of the House Judiciary Committee.

Chief Justice William H. Rehnquist caused a buzz when he showed up for the trial. He wore the

Chief Justice Rehnquist swears in
all one hundred senators as jurors for
the impeachment trial.

traditional black judge's robe, but for this special occasion his robe had four bright gold stripes at the shoulder. The Chief Justice had designed the robe himself from a costume he had seen in a Gilbert and Sullivan operetta.

Since there were no hard and fast rules about how a senatorial trial should proceed, the Senate had to make up many of the rules as it went along. The most important fight was over witnesses. The managers wanted to present at least fifteen live witnesses. The president's defenders didn't want any. They countered by saying if the managers were allowed to have a large number of witnesses the defense would also ask to present a long list of witnesses, and the trial would drag on for months. Then "the genie is out of the bottle," presidential lawyer David Kendall warned.

A long trial was the last thing that the Senate wanted. In addition, senators were openly horrified by the prospect of Monica Lewinsky sitting in the senate chamber and describing her sexual activities with the president in graphic detail. As a face-saving compromise, the Senate allowed the managers to have only three witnesses. And they were not to appear live. They were to be deposed by both sides, and taped portions of the depositions could be shown during the presentations made at the trial. The House managers were bitterly disappointed, and said so. Henry Hyde called the number of witnesses "a pitiful three."

The final choice of witnesses was interesting and reveals a good deal about the political nature of the trial. Monica Lewinsky was, for obvious reasons, at the top of the witness list. The second witness was Vernon Jordan, again an obvious choice. The third was Sidney Blumenthal.

Blumenthal was a surprise. He was an assistant to the president and a fierce political operative. He was reported to have told people that the president was innocent and that Lewinsky was a "stalker" who had pursued Bill Clinton. If the president had told this to his assistant, and instructed him to spread the story, that might have constituted obstruction of justice—but it was a stretch. At best Blumenthal was a minor player.

A far more obvious witness would have been Betty Currie, the president's secretary. She was the person Lewinsky was supposed to be visiting when she came to the White House. She was the one who picked up the gifts from Lewinsky. But Betty Currie was a popular and likable person whose only sin may have been excessive loyalty to her boss.

Betty Currie was also an African American, as was Vernon Jordan. Polls showed that African Americans as a group were Bill Clinton's strongest supporters, and in the House it was black representatives who led the president's defense. To have two of only three witnesses black, and then to have them questioned by House managers who were all white males—many of them southerners—might have looked like persecution.

Blumenthal, a sharp-tongued, white, male, political operator with many enemies, was not the sort of witness people were going to feel sorry for. If he didn't have much to add to the managers' case, at least he wasn't going to hurt it with the public.

As things turned out the House managers may have been lucky that they did not have Lewinsky testify in public. They might have expected the public to see a sad and vulnerable young woman telling a tale of how she had been wronged by her predatory boss who happened to be the president.

By the time of the Senate trial Monica Lewinsky had told her story often and was quite comfortable and confident with it. She was no longer the unhappy young woman who had poured her heart out to Linda Tripp or broken down in hysterical fits of weeping when confronted by the FBI.

Newsweek reported that during an informal interview with the House impeachment trial managers, "Lewinsky was cool and at times, slightly mocking toward the prosecutors. At one point, Representative Bill McCollum of Florida was asking Lewinsky about her involvement with the president. Monica eyed the starched and prim McCollum and coyly answered, 'I don't want to put a wrinkle in your shirt.'"[1]

Her formal taped deposition was, if anything, even less helpful to prosecutors. Lewinsky stood by her statement that no one had asked her to lie or offered her a job in exchange for her false affidavit. She refused to agree that the president was lying when his testimony contradicted hers, conceding only that her memory or interpretation differed from his. And she said that she still respected and admired the president. Prosecutors didn't fare much better with Jordan or Blumenthal.

The trial formally began on January 14. Early in the proceedings forty-four senators, all Democrats, voted that the case be dismissed outright. Only Democrat Russell Feingold of Wisconsin voted against dismissal. That motion failed, but since sixty-seven out of one hundred senators were needed to convict, it was clear that the votes for conviction simply were not there. All the suspense went out of the trial.

Despite the many obstacles and setbacks, the House managers presented a very credible case. But it was also a familiar case. Nothing new had been added. The president's defenders, led by lawyer Charles Ruff, were skillful in their defense. But their arguments were also very familiar. No senatorial minds were being changed. Polls indicated that a substantial majority of the public had long ago made up its mind that President Clinton should not be removed from office, and nothing that was happening in the Senate had altered that. In fact, the public wasn't even that interested anymore.

Time painted a bleak picture for the House trial managers:

Suddenly the [senate] chamber resembled nothing so much as a classroom full of kids waiting for the bell to ring. "It's like final exams are just about over," says Gordon Smith, Republican of Oregon. "We're all anxious to head for the exits."

The only people not sharing the good vibes were the 13 House trial managers, many of whom sat at their table with bloodshot eyes and puffy faces, looking like members of some unwanted and unforgiven tribe of outcasts. Their White House counterparts move easily among the Senators, clutching elbows and exchanging meaningful looks, while the House managers have become pariahs—"two-year-olds," as a G.O.P. Senator disdainfully described them in a private meeting with his colleagues. "And everyone knows you shouldn't give two-year-olds everything they want."[2]

After the presentations the senators voted to conduct their deliberations behind closed doors. These deliberations were not exactly secret, for as soon as a session ended, senators rushed to the nearest television camera to give their versions of what had been said. By having the actual discussions held off camera, Senate leaders hoped that their colleagues would be able to resist grandstanding or taking too much time and delaying the much hoped-for end.

In general the senators seemed pleased with this arrangement. Most of them described the sessions as dignified, thoughtful, frank, and open, yet friendly and nonpartisan. The implied contrast with the much criticized House debate was unstated but obvious.

The final vote, which was public, came on February 13, 1999. It was anticlimactic. The only suspense was the exact vote total. The Democrats stuck together, and ten Republicans abandoned the GOP and voted against convicting the president of perjury (making the vote 55–45 against); five Republicans voted "not guilty" on obstruction of justice, a 50–50 tie. Neither count had commanded even a simple majority, much less the two thirds needed to convict. In the end it wasn't even close.

Attempts to couple the acquittal with a censure or some other form of showing disapproval of the president's behavior without actually removing him from office collapsed. Everything that could have been said already had been said. The senators just wanted to head for the exit, and they did.

It had been a little over a year since the story of the president and the former intern first burst upon the scene. Now the impeachment of William Jefferson Clinton was over.

11

Legacy

Over at the White House news of the acquittal was greeted with an almost eerie silence. Bill Clinton was not smoking cigars or banging drums. No champagne corks were popping. There were no impromptu parties, not even a lot of backslapping and high fives in the corridors. Whatever the president and his aides felt privately, a strenuous effort had been made not to gloat or even look very happy.

The president stepped out into the Rose Garden, alone, in front of a rather sullen press corps and spoke very briefly. He said that he was "profoundly sorry [for] what I said and did to trigger these events." He vowed to lead the nation toward "reconciliation and renewal." Then he went back into the White House to write thank-you notes to some of his supporters.

THE IRAQ BOMBINGS ■ McGWIRE UP CLOSE ■ HILLARY'S YEAR

MEN OF THE YEAR
KENNETH STARR AND BILL CLINTON

THE IMPEACHMENT
OF THE PRESIDENT 1998

According to *Time* managing editor Walter Isaacson, the decision to name both Clinton and Starr as Men of the Year was easier once Clinton was acquitted.

In June 1999, Bob Woodward (the Watergate reporter and now an editor at *The Washington Post*) published the book *Shadow* about presidential scandals since Watergate. Woodward is one of the most influential and well-connected journalists in Washington. More than half of the book was devoted to President Clinton. In the book he paints a picture of a despondent and brooding president, isolated from his family, his staff, and his party. He felt that no one had ever had his private life made so public.

Even acquittal by the Senate was viewed as a hollow victory. "I'll survive," the president is quoted as saying, "but I'll never be the same."[1]

Bill Clinton didn't win the impeachment fight—he merely survived. There were no winners and no heroes.

It is still far too early to judge the full impact of the events of 1998. But a few things are already clear.

The whole process was so distasteful that it doomed the Office of Independent Counsel to extinction. In May 1999 the Watergate-era law that created the office was allowed to lapse. During congressional hearings on the law even Kenneth Starr himself testified against it. How future allegations of presidential misbehavior will be handled is not yet known.

Clinton's Republican opponents were clear losers. They lost two Speakers of the House, and polls showed that the party's popularity—especially for representatives and senators—had dropped sharply on the national level. This was felt most keenly by social conservatives, most of whom had energetically supported the Republican party.

In February 1999, Paul M. Weyrich, president of the Free Congress Foundation, the man who had originally suggested the term "Moral Majority," and one of the most influential ideological leaders of the conservative movement, posted "An Open Letter to Conservatives Following the Senate Impeachment Vote" on his Web site.

Weyrich's tone was despairing: "If there really were a moral majority out there Bill Clinton would have been driven out of office months ago," he wrote.

"I think it is that politics itself has failed. And politics has failed because of the collapse of the culture. The culture we are living in becomes an ever-wider sewer. In truth, I think we are caught up in a cultural collapse of historic proportions, a collapse so great that it simply overwhelms politics."[2]

His suggestion was that conservatives should drop out of politics entirely and as much as possible drop out of modern American culture.

Not all conservatives shared Weyrich's deep pessimism, but many echoed his view that Bill Clinton's survival was a sure sign that conservatives had lost "the culture war."

Bill Clinton came out of the impeachment crisis a severely wounded president with a tarnished legacy. He had desperately wanted to be remembered as the president who had led America into the twenty-first century. He was more likely to be remembered as the only twentieth-century president to be impeached. No matter how history would finally judge the record of his two terms in office, the name Monica Lewinsky would always come up.

He lost a full year of his presidency to the scandal. Despite repeated claims by Clinton loyalists that the president had a remarkable ability to "compartmentalize" and not let himself be distracted by the scandal that nearly consumed him, it is now clear that not only the president but the entire Clinton administration was seriously distracted during 1998. Fortunately for America the year was a prosperous and relatively peaceful one—there were no major domestic or foreign crises to deal with. But many problems from education to health care and social security were allowed to fester.

For the remainder of his term Clinton would have to deal with a Congress where more than half the members didn't believe that he deserved to be in office, and tried to block many of his programs, and where even his friends no longer trusted his word.

Two months after the president was acquitted by the Senate, the judge in the Paula Jones lawsuit found him guilty of contempt for giving "false, misleading and evasive answers that were designed to obstruct the judicial process." In August, Bill Clinton was fined $90,000 for lying in the Jones case. That was just the start, for there was little doubt that even after he left office President Clinton would face years of expensive and nagging legal troubles.

And there would be nonlegal troubles as well, the inevitable embarrassing revelations from former aides and associates, perhaps accusations from other women, and the constant jokes. In May 1999, Monica Lewinsky herself appeared on *Saturday Night Live* in two skits, one with Clinton impersonator Darrell Hammond.[3]

Linda Tripp was another major loser. Most surveys indicated that she was the least popular figure in the case. In August 1999 Tripp was indicted in Maryland for taping her conversations with Monica Lewinsky. Secretly recording telephone conversations is illegal in the state of Maryland, where Tripp lived.

The effects of the Lewinsky matter on the career of Hillary Rodham Clinton will be determined as time goes by. Mrs. Clinton was both admired and pitied by the public as the scandal unfolded. Her popularity rose sharply. By early 1999 she seriously began to consider running for the seat of retiring New York Senator Daniel Patrick Moynihan. Though she had not officially announced her candidacy, she immediately became the front-runner for the nomination.

Press interest in her probable candidacy was enormous. The one question that seemed to most intrigue people was, "Why don't you leave him?" Hillary Clinton tried to answer the question in an interview given to *Talk* magazine. She said that she and her husband still loved one another very much, and that her husband's actions had been "sins of weakness." She went on to say that Bill Clinton's early life was "scarred by abuse . . . there was a terrible conflict between his mother and grandmother."

Whatever else Hillary Rodham Clinton might have to say about any other subject was totally swept away by the tidal wave of attention paid to these few remarks. She was both praised and ridiculed, and the controversy dominated the tabloids and political talk shows. Facing a barrage of media questions during a New York campaign swing, Mrs. Clinton said she just wasn't going to talk about the subject anymore.

Interestingly, the media was yet another casualty of the events of 1998. Even though the public often devoured all the tawdry details, the media was widely blamed for presenting so much information, and generally lowering the tone of the coverage. Many reporters and editors in the mainstream media were also worried about the role they played. Had they gone too far in exposing the private life of an individual—even if he happened to be president of the United States? Were they becoming more like the tabloids they sneered at?

Michael Isikoff, the *Newsweek* reporter who had done so much to uncover the Lewinsky scandal, wrote of how, as a college student in the early 1970s, he was inspired by the reporting of Bob Woodward and Carl Bernstein of *The Washington Post,* who had done so much to uncover the crimes of the Nixon administration. A whole generation of journalists was inspired by Woodward and Bernstein. It is doubtful if the next generation of journalists will be inspired by Michael Isikoff.[4]

Most of all, the American people lost. The cynicism and mistrust of national leaders, which had become so much a part of the national scene since Watergate, was on the rise again. The American people lost trust in and respect for their elected leaders.

The most serious international crisis of 1998 came near the end of the year, while the impeachment hearings were going on in the House. The long-simmering conflict with Iraq's Saddam Hussein flared up into a major bombing campaign. This was the most intense action since the Gulf War of the Bush administration, and by far the largest military action undertaken by President Bill Clinton.

The Iraqis and their supporters claimed that the bombing campaign, called Desert Fox, was an American trick, designed to divert attention from the Lewinsky scandal.

That charge was echoed by some of the president's domestic critics. They suggested that what was going on in Iraq was sort of a *Wag the Dog* scenario. *Wag the Dog* is a 1997 film about a scandal-plagued president whose political "fixer" recruits a hotshot Hollywood producer to stage a nonexistent war to distract the public. Bill Clinton, with his scandal, his team of political advisers, many Hollywood friends, and now his small war, seemed a perfect match for the president in the film.

In the end the country certainly survived the scandal. Even the creaky and cumbersome institution of impeachment worked the way it was supposed to. But there was really nothing to cheer about.

Everybody lost.

Chronology

1995   June: Monica Lewinsky becomes White House intern.

November 15: Lewinsky has first sexual encounter with President Bill Clinton.

December: Lewinsky hired to work full-time at White House.

1996   April: Lewinsky reassigned to job at Pentagon. Meets Linda Tripp.

November: Clinton reelected.

1997   October 3: Tripp begins taping phone calls with Lewinsky.

December 19: Lewinsky subpoenaed by Paula Jones's lawyers.

December 28: Clinton and Lewinsky have last meeting.

1998   January 7: Lewinsky files affidavit in Jones case denying sexual relations with the president.

January 12: Tripp tells Kenneth Starr's investigators about tapes.

January 13: Wired by FBI, Tripp meets Lewinsky at Ritz-Carlton Hotel.

January 16: Lewinsky detained by FBI.

January 17: Clinton gives deposition to Paula Jones's lawyers.

January 19: Drudge Report breaks scandal story on the Internet.

January 26: Clinton forcefully assures nation, "I did not have sexual relations with that woman—Miss Lewinsky."

April 1: Paula Jones's lawsuit dismissed.

August 6: Lewinsky appears before Starr grand jury for the first time.

August 17: Clinton testifies before grand jury via closed-circuit television.

September 9: Starr Report delivered to Congress.

September 11: Starr Report made public.

September 21: House Judiciary Committee releases videotape of Clinton's grand-jury testimony.

October 8: House authorizes impeachment inquiry.

November: Republicans suffer losses in midterm elections.

December 19: House votes to impeach the president.

1999   February 13: Senate votes not to remove the president from office.

Notes

Chapter One
1. *Newsweek*, February 2, 1998, p. 45.

Chapter Three
1. *Newsweek*, p. 28.
2. Michael Isikoff, *Uncovering Clinton: A Reporter's Story* (New York: Crown, 1999), pp. 192–193.
3. Ibid., p. 190.
4. Ibid., p. 196.

Chapter Four
1. Isikoff, p. 237.
2. Ibid., p. 266.
3. Ibid., p. 279.

Chapter Five
1. Isikoff, pp. 315–316.
2. *Newsweek*, p. 45.

Chapter Six
1. *Time,* January 26, 1998, p. 24.
2. *Newsweek*, p. 29.
3. Ibid., p. 50.
4. *The Washington Post*, May 2, 1999, p. A24.

Chapter Seven
1. *Mclean's Magazine*, August 17, 1998, p. 30.
2. *U.S. News & World* Report, June 22, 1998, p. 40.
3. William J. Bennett, *The Death of Outrage: Bill Clinton and the Assault on American Ideals* (New York: The Free Press, 1998), p. 133.

Chapter Eight
1. *The Starr Report* (New York: Pocket Books, 1998), Back Cover.
2. Ibid., p. 22.
3. *Mclean's Magazine*, October 5, 1998, p. 24.

Chapter Nine
1. Knight Ridder/Tribune News Service, January 13, 1999.

Chapter Ten
1. *Newsweek*, February 8, 1999, p. 22.
2. *Time*, February 15, 1999, p. 30.

Chapter Eleven
1. Bob Woodward, "A President's Isolation," *The Washington Post* (June 13, 1999), p. A1.
2. *CulturalDissident*, http://www.culturaldissident. com/logs/Paul6.htm
3. Associated Press, May 10, 1999.
4. Isikoff, p. 8.

Bibliography

Bennett, William J. *The Death of Outrage: Bill Clinton and the Assault on American Ideals.* New York: The Free Press, 1998.

Bugliosi, Vincent. *No Island of Sanity: Paula Jones v. Bill Clinton in the Supreme Court.* New York: Ballantine, 1998.

Cwiklik, Robert. *Bill Clinton: Our 42nd President.* Brookfield, CT: The Millbrook Press, 1993.

Isikoff, Michael. *Uncovering Clinton: A Reporter's Story.* New York: Crown, 1999.

Kurtz, Howard. *Spin Cycle: Inside the Clinton Propaganda Machine.* New York: The Free Press, 1998.

Maraniss, David. *First in His Class: A Biography of Bill Clinton.* New York: Simon & Schuster, 1995.

Morton, Andrew. *Monica's Story.* New York: St. Martin's Press, 1999.

The Starr Report: The Independent Counsel's Complete Report to Congress on the Investigation of President Clinton. New York: Pocket Books, 1998.

Stephanopoulos, George. *All Too Human: A Political Education.* Boston: Little, Brown, 1999.

Strauss, Stephen D. *The Complete Idiot's Guide to the Impeachment of the President.* New York: Alpha Books, 1998.

Woodward, Bob. *Shadow: Five Presidents and the Legacy of Watergate.* New York: Simon & Schuster, 1999.

Index

Page numbers in *italics* refer to illustrations.

Aldrich, Gary, 24, 28
American Spectator, The, 54

Barr, Bob, 51, 53, 81–82
Bennett, Bob, 31, 65
Bennett, William J., 65
Bernstein, Carl, 102
Blumenthal, Sidney, 91–93
Book of Virtues, The (W.J.
   Bennett), 65
Bradlee, Ben, 11
Bush, George, 23

Cacheris, Plato, 65
Civil War, 79
Cleveland, Grover, 10
Clinton, Bill, *35*, *97*
   aftermath of impeachment
     crisis and, 99–100, 103
   draft and, 15
   enemies of, 16–17, 54, 73
   Flowers episode and, 13–15,
     30, 53

Clinton, Bill *(continued)*
   Foster suicide and, 17, 54
   grand-jury testimony of,
     66–68, 72–73
   impeachment of, 74, 77–95
   Jones case and, 18, 20, 21,
     30, 34, 35, 37–39, 47, 49,
     64, 85, 100
   Lewinsky, relationship with,
     7–10, 12, 26–27, 49–51,
     52, 53, 55, 56, 66, 68
   marijuana experiences of, 15
   political views of, 16
   presidential campaign
     (1992) of, 13–14
   presidential campaign
     (1996) of, 17, 51
   public opinion and, 55, 64,
     73–74
   Sixty Minutes interview
     and, 15, 56
   Starr Report and, 69–72, 74
   State of the Union message
     (1998) of, 56–57, 64
   Whitewater case and, 21–22
   Willey charges and, 24, 37

Clinton, Hillary Rodham, 15, 21, 53, 54, 56, *57*, 101–102
Clinton Chronicles, The (video), 17
Congressional election (1998), 74–76
Conservative Action Political Committee, 18
Currie, Betty, 37–38, *39*, 45, 48–49, 60, 91–9

Death of Outrage, The: Bill Clinton and the Assault on American Ideals (W.J. Bennett), 65
DeLay, Tom, 85
Drudge, Matt, 7–8, *9*
Drudge Report, 7–8

Executive privilege, 6

Falwell, Jerry, 17
Feingold, Russell, 93
Fifth Amendment to the Constitution, 59

Fiske, Robert, 22
Flowers, Gennifer, 13–15, 30, 53
Flynt, Larry, 81, 85
Foster, Vincent, 17, 24, 54
Fox, Fannie, 11

Gephardt, Richard, *80*
Gingrich, Newt, 69, 76, 84
Ginsberg, William, 46, 50, 61–62, 65
Goldberg, Lucianne, 27–30, 40, 54
Grand jury hearings, 58–62, 65–68, 72–74

Hammond, Darrell, 100
Harding, Warren G., 10
Hart, Gary, 11
Hays, Wayne, 11
Hill, Anita, 12
Hussein, Saddam, 103
Hyde, Henry, 81, 88, 90

Impeachment proceedings, 74, 77–95

Isikoff, Michael, 9–10, 28, 30, 48, 102

Johnson, Andrew, 78–79
Jones, Paula, 18, 20, 21
    case brought by, 30, 34–35, 37–39, 47, 49, 64, 85, 100
Jordan, Vernon, 9, 34, *35*, 37, 38, 40, 45, 91, 93
Justice Department, 21

Kendall, David, 82–83, 90
Kennedy, John F., 10–11
King, Larry, 62

Lewinsky, Bernard, 46
Lewinsky, Monica, *36*
    aftermath of impeachment crisis and, 100
    Clinton, relationship with, 7–10, 12, 26–27, 49–51, *52*, 53, 55, 56, 66, 68
    FBI interview of, 41–43
    gifts from Clinton, 37–38
    grand-jury testimony of, 65–66, 74
    impeachment of Clinton and, 90, 92–93
    Jones case and, 34–35, 37–39
    letters of, 29, *32–33*
    Office of the Independent Counsel and, 42–43, 45–46
    Starr Report and, 70, 74
    Tripp and, 26–30, 35, 37, 40–41, 43
Lewis, Marcia, 34, 45, 46, 50, 60
Lieberman, Evelyn, 26
Lincoln, Abraham, 79
Livingood, William, 69
Livingston, Bob, 84–85

McCollum, Bill, 92–93
McDougal, Jim, 22
McDougal, Susan, 22
McGovern, George, 27
Mills, Wilbur, 11
Moynihan, Daniel Patrick, 101

National Enquirer, 11

Newsweek magazine, 8–10, 28, 47–48, 53, 92, 102
New York Times, The, 55, 62, 73
Nixon, Richard, 21, 50, 54, 79

Office of the Independent Counsel, 21, 22, 38, 40–43, 45–46, 50, 61–63, 65–70, 82, 98

Packwood, Bob, 12
Pepperdine University, 54

Ray, Elizabeth, 11
Reagan, Ronald, 21
Rehnquist, William H., 88, *89*, 90
Revlon Corporation, 38
Rice, Donna, 11
Roosevelt, Franklin D., 51, 75
Ruff, Charles, 93

Scaife, Richard Mellon, 54–55
Seventeenth Amendment to the Constitution, 88
Shadow (Woodward), 98
Sixty Minutes (CBS), 15, 56
Smith, Gordon, 94
Smith, Richard M., 10
Starr, Kenneth, 21, 22, 43, *44*, 54, 58, 60, 64, 68, 69, 73, 74, 82, *97*, 98

Starr Report, 69–72, *71*, 74
State of the Union message (1998), 56–57, 64
Stein, Jacob, 65
Stephanopoulos, George, 53

This Week (ABC), 8
Thomas, Clarence, 12
Time magazine, 49, 94, *97*
Tripp, Linda, 22–24, *25*, 26–30, 35, 37, 38, 40–41, 50, 54, 60–61, 66, 92, 101
Tucker, Jim Guy, 22

Unlimited Access (Aldrich), 24, 28

Vanity Fair magazine, 62

Wag the Dog (film), 103
Washington Post, The, 8–9, 55, 62, 98, 102
Watergate, 21, 43, 50, 98
Weyrich, Paul M., 99
Whitewater, 21–22
Willey, Kathleen, 24, 37
Woodward, Bob, 98, 102
Wright, Susan Webber, 64

Zogby, John, 74